DUKE
SUCKS

DUKE SUCKS

A COMPLETELY EVENHANDED,
UNBIASED INVESTIGATION INTO THE
MOST EVIL TEAM ON PLANET EARTH

REED TUCKER &
ANDY BAGWELL

FOREWORD BY IAN WILLIAMS

ST. MARTIN'S GRIFFIN
NEW YORK

www.stmartins.com

Library of Congress Cataloging-in-Publication Data

Tucker, Reed.
    Duke sucks : a completely evenhanded, unbiased investigation into the most evil team on planet earth / Reed Tucker and Andy Bagwell.
        p. cm.
    ISBN 978-1-250-00463-5 (pbk.)
    ISBN 978-1-250-00819-0 (e-book)
    1. Duke Blue Devils (Basketball team)—Humor.   2. Duke University—Basketball—Humor.   I. Bagwell, Andy.   II. Title.
    GV885.43.D85T83 2012
    796.323'6309756563—dc23

                                                              2011038063

10 9 8 7 6 5 4 3 2

With apologies to our Duke friends, of which
we have many. Or used to.

CONTENTS

Acknowledgments   xi

Foreword by Ian Williams   xiii

Introduction   1

Charge #1   5
Duke is dirtier than a bus station bathroom floor.

Charge #2   11
The annoying, pointless floor slap.

Exhibit A   15
Graduation Rates

Charge #3   16
The only way the tournament selection committee could give Duke an easier road to the Final Four every year would be to draw them a map.

Charge #4   23
Their mascot is incredibly lame. And worse, French.

Exhibit B   27
Top 5 Duke Scandals

Charge #5   31
The word "lifetime" evidently doesn't mean the same thing to Coach K as it does to the rest of us.

Charge #6   37
Duke is where big men's careers go to die.

CONTENTS

Charge #7   43
Duke causes cancer.

Exhibit C   48
J. J. Redick's Poetry

Charge #8   50
Dookies are fair-weather fans who cannot be counted on
when their teams get down.

Charge #9   56
[This charge has been redacted for fear that Coach K
might call us and scorch the earth with F-bombs for
twenty minutes.]

Charge #10   63
Duke would not play a true road game against a quality
opponent if Coach K's vertebrae depended on it.

Exhibit D   68
Top 12 Most Humiliating Moments

Charge #11   74
The media are a bunch of slobbering, pro–Blue Devils fools who
lay awake nights fantasizing about running their fingers through
Coach K's downy toupee.

Charge #12   80
Coach K uses six pounds of lampblack on his hair per week.

Charge #13   84
"The Stomp" managed to encapsulate everything we hate about
Duke in a single, awful moment: dickish behavior, an entitled
mentality, preferential treatment, selective memory loss by the media,
and floppy hair.

CONTENTS

Exhibit E   90
Match-the-Quote Game

Charge #14   93
Duke's coaching tree is not exactly a mighty oak.

Charge #15   98
*Duke is paranoid, and it can feel your hate
breathing on the back of its neck, all wet and hot and
smelling of ribs sauce.*

Charge #16   104
*Duke students are a bunch of wealthy, elitist punks who you
probably wouldn't want to get stuck talking to at the polo match.*

Exhibit F   110
Duke's All-Overpaid NBA Team

Charge #17   112
Duke gets more calls than a Mumbai customer-service center.

Charge #18   119
The school's architecture sucks.

Exhibit G   124
The Elton Brand E-mail

Charge #19   127
Duke players in the NBA are not exactly setting the world on fire.

Charge #20   131
Duke flops worse than a latter-day Nic Cage movie.

Charge #21   136
*The Cameron Crazies ain't all they're cracked up to be. Clap,
clap, clap-clap-clap.*

CONTENTS

Charge #22   144
Duke is most hated in its own backyard.

Charge #23   151
Coach K is too good to autograph anything for you.

Exhibit H   153
Why Your Team Hates Duke

Charge #24   157
Coach K's program has had more defectors than Cuba.

Charge #25   161
Gimme a P! Gimme an L! Gimme an A! Gimme an I!
Gimme an N!

Exhibit I   165
Frankendookie

Charge #26   166
Gaaaaaaaaaaaaaak.

Exhibit J   170
Top 11 Most Hated Duke Players (Because a List of 10
Was Just Not Enough)

Charge #∞   179

Afterword   181

ACKNOWLEDGMENTS

Special thanks to Jonathan Jones and Adrian Atkinson.

FOREWORD

BY IAN WILLIAMS

The best thing about hating Duke University is that you never have to explain yourself. Back in 2004, when I made a few T-shirts that said I HATED DOOK BEFORE HATING DOOK WAS COOL, nobody asked, "Wait, why do you hate Duke?" It's one of those things—like nausea, acne, and wasps—we can all agree on.

Of course, there will always be the hermetic shut-in who has no sense of history or drama, and who thinks any such animosity is, at best, childish—and at worst, close-mindedly tribal. They might lump our rivalry in with all other school rivalries, seeing no difference between us and the tailgating yahoos from institutions like Alabama cheering against Auburn, their distended bellies wobbling as they scream epithets over charred hot dogs.

There are many reasons—philosophical, socioeconomic, aesthetic—why our rivalry transcends all others, but let's just keep it simple: Alabama and Auburn hate Duke, too.

In 1990, I wrote a piece in the University of North Carolina's student paper *The Daily Tar Heel* about why I found that school in Durham so execrable. I thought it was such a forgone conclusion, and so eye-rollingly obvious, that the UNC column would be quickly forgotten. Instead, it "went viral," which, three years before the Internet came to Carolina, meant it was cut out of the newspaper and pasted onto thousands of dorm doors, office cubicles, and refrigerators. Now I get it forwarded to me every February like clockwork.

But why? Why does the disgust bubble up like acid reflux, year after year? In September 1948, my roommate's dad and his friends took some winter wheat seeds and planted an interlocking "NC" on Duke's football field. By November, there was a North Carolina logo on the 50-yard-line they couldn't erase. Why did they do that? Have you ever heard of someone hating, say, Wake Forest that much?

You couldn't have two better guides than Andy Bagwell and Reed Tucker, who will spend the rest of this book diving—nay, plunging—into the netherworld of Dook hatred. But I'll venture a guess: consistent dickishness and recurrent douchebaggery. And you need look no further than through the eyes of a child to see it.

In 2007, my daughter Lucy was two, and we had flown to Chapel Hill to see the UNC–Duke game at the Dean Dome. She dressed up like a two-foot-five-inch Tyler Hansbrough with a toddler-size number 50 jersey the size of a dinner napkin, and stayed home to watch the game with the babysitter while my wife and I experienced the glorious ass-kicking in person.

You might remember, however, the final seconds: Tyler's nose "got in the way" of Gerald Henderson's swinging fist, sending him to the ground in a spray of blood, with the fan base ready to riot. Coach K completed the evening by saying Gerald "was the real victim here."

When we were reunited with Lucy, she was wide-eyed and devastated at what she'd just seen on television. I didn't want to freak her out, and you want your kids to believe in a fairly moral universe, so I tried to answer her questions.

"Did Tyler get hurt bad?" she asked.

"Yes, sweetie, his nose is broken."

"Did the Dook man say he sorry for Tyler fall down?"

"Well, no. He blamed Coach Roy for leaving Tyler in the game."

And in one instant, a seedling called "shock" is planted, which grows into the sapling of "disgust," and eventually into the tree of "hatred." I don't need any propaganda; Lucy is six now, and I heard her sing *"Go to Hell, Dook!"* in the bathtub last night.

Loathing Duke University requires no exposition; everyone gets it. It beareth all things, believeth all things, endureth all things. It is as perennial as the grass. Hating Duke is never having to say you're sorry.

Ian Williams lives in both New York, New York, and Venice, California, and writes for television and film with his wife, Tessa Blake. Both bleed Carolina blue, and God willin', so will their six-year-old daughter, Lucy.

"I'm going to get rid of my jacket. It's warm in here. Reggie, would you take this? This is Reggie Love—he's from Duke. Any Duke fans here?"

Scattered boos.

"Uh-oh."

—Barack Obama at a 2008 Pennsylvania campaign stop

DUKE
SUCKS

INTRODUCTION

L et's get this out there in the open.

We, your humble coauthors, are horribly biased. We are both graduates of the University of North Carolina (UNC) at Chapel Hill, and we have been perfectly engineered, much like a cyborg in a bad sci-fi movie, to loathe everything in royal blue. We have owned anti-Duke T-shirts portraying Coach Mike Krzyzewski (Coach K) as a rat. We have screamed horrific slurs at Christian Laettner that have made small children cry. One crisp fall evening, we found ourselves driving around Durham with a burlap sack, some rope, and a shovel, looking for J. J. Redick's house. Allegedly.

So, okay, fine. You got us. We don't like Duke.

But the strange thing is, the more we investigated the hatred of Duke's basketball team, the more we discovered that we were not alone. This is not some pocket conspiracy cooked up by Tar Heels fans. Duke hatred is a truly global phenomenon—an unprecedented worldwide outpouring of ill will toward five dorky guys who dribble a basketball.

According to Google, users searched for variations on "Hate Duke" or "Duke Sucks" more than 8,300 times in March 2011. Cruder fans searched for "Fuck Duke" an astonishing 18,690 times per month.

On Facebook, a group called "I Hate It When I Wake Up and Duke Still Exists" has (at last count) 17,028 likes. Another, called less poetically "Duke Losing," has 6,757.

There's more.

Back in 2005, MSNBC conducted a poll of the most hated

team in college basketball. The Blue Devils came out on top with an unbelievable 53 percent. Landslide doesn't even begin to describe it. The second-place team, UNC, pulled well up the rear with just 18 percent.

In 2010, cable channel Spike TV anointed Duke as its number one "least likeable team," fuming, "I'm pretty sure Duke is the official team of both child murderers and Asian dictators."

Bottom line: Unless you went to Duke, you don't like Duke. It's as simple as that.

No team in all of sports—college or professional—is as uniquely hated as those smug, entitled, floor-slapping, fist-pumping, chest-thumping, insufferable Blue Devils.

"ABD!" (Anybody But Duke) goes a popular mantra. Please, God, Jesus, Buddha, and Tom Cruise OT Level VII Scientologist—anybody but Duke.

According to a *USA Today* poll, 49 percent of viewers actively rooted against the Devils in the 2010 national championship game.

A Match.com survey discovered that 5 percent of hard-up singles still wouldn't date someone who rooted for the Blue Devils.

In 2010, even Fox's TV show *Glee*—not exactly a show for sports fans—got into the act when one of its characters exclaimed, "I hate Duke like I hate the Nazis!"

An *Esquire* writer touring through a remote part of Zaire in 1996 reported that he came across a young boy wearing a DUKE SUCKS T-shirt.

This is hardly just a Duke–North Carolina thing. Something else is going on here.

The most common explanation is that people dislike the Blue Devils because they succeed. "I think the guys in the past have put that upon us," Duke forward Lance Thomas explained at the 2010 Final Four. "Just with the success they've had."

Coach Mike Krzyzewski himself offered the same rationale when asked in March 2011 why his university seems unusually loathed.

"We're as popular of a team as there is in the United States," he told a radio show. "But we're also a hated team because we have won."

Okay, not to nitpick, but he only said two things in that quote, and he got both of them wrong.

Duke is not "as popular of a team as there is in the United States." If you want to go by merchandise sales, and that seems as clear as any method to measure something abstract like popularity, Duke is about as popular as dengue fever. According to the Collegiate Licensing Company, Duke in 2010 did not even finish in the Top 25 when it came to sales of T-shirts, workout gear, and other licensed goods. It was beaten soundly by conference-mates UNC, Florida State, and even Clemson.

But on to the more important point: K's reasoning for why Duke is hated.

This tired "we've won" argument has been offered over the years by hundreds of fans and a handful of deluded sports columnists, but it crumbles under the barest of scrutiny. College basketball is loaded with teams that win, both historically and season-to-season. UCLA has by far the most championships, but you don't see anyone printing up anti-Bruin T-shirts by the millions. Kentucky is the winningest program in college basketball history, and it hasn't exactly spawned a cottage industry worth roughly the GDP of a small island nation aimed at tearing it apart.

No, something else is going on to explain all this hatred, and we humbly submit that so many people hate Duke because Duke deserves to be hated.

Where there's smoke, there's fire.

Some institutions and people are just vile—the Taliban, Kim Jong-il, Jay Leno—and through their behavior and demeanor, they correctly engender a hatred in most logical human beings.

Millions of basketball fans around the world are not imagining things. Duke really is evil, and we will prove it.

And we'll do it, not just by juvenilely calling them names or making fun of their players' hair—although that's fun, too—but by presenting an airtight, objective case against them that would stand up in a court of law.

There's not enough paper in the world to cover every stone thrown at the Devils, so we'll present a choice few.

Bailiff, bring on the charges!

CHARGE #1

DUKE IS DIRTIER THAN A BUS STATION BATHROOM FLOOR.

I know for a fact that that was not by accident."

That's UNC guard Dewey Burke's take on one of the most infamous plays in Duke basketball history. March 4, 2007. Chapel Hill, North Carolina. With 14.5 seconds left in an eventual 86–72 UNC victory, Carolina's Tyler Hansbrough retrieves his own miss from the foul line and goes up for a putback. Suddenly, Duke's Gerald Henderson comes swooping in from behind and smashes his elbow into Hansbrough's face, breaking the star player's nose and sending blood gushing down his mug, across his uniform, and onto the floor.

"I can't tell you how I know that or details, but I know that was not an accident," says Burke, who was on the court during the play and held Hansbrough back from charging Henderson. "That was supposed to happen. I don't think they were trying to break Tyler's nose or wanted him to bleed like that, but they were trying to send some sort of message of, 'We're not going out like this.'"

Everyone involved, including both coaches, claimed in the postgame press conference that the elbow was an accident. (Though Coach K would snidely suggest that it was partially UNC coach Roy Williams's fault for leaving his starters on the floor so late in the game.)

"But look, we were gonna take the high road and say, 'Hey, we knew it wasn't on purpose, and we're moving on,'" Burke says. "But all of us in the program knew there was a lot more to it than that."

Dirty is a tough thing to prove. One man's "hard foul" is another man's "assault and battery." Anyone who's hooped on the playgrounds is familiar with the "no blood, no foul" rule, but Duke seems to take it a bit too literally sometimes.

While no one can prove that Duke is out to play dirty basketball, the trail of blood, bruises, and broken bones the team has left in its wake would seem to speak for itself.

There will be blood, all right. Lots of blood. So much blood that a game will look like an episode of *CSI: Durham*.

Let's go back a few decades and peer deep into the history of Duke dirtiness, all the way back to the 1930s, shortly after the school became Duke University.

"Duke was preparing to play North Carolina. Concerned with UNC's big center 'Tiny' Harper, Bill Werber and Harry Councillor practiced throwing a ball at the head of Duke center Joe Crosson, who would duck as the ball approached him," Jim Sumner wrote in his book, *Tales from the Duke Blue Devils Hardwood*. "At the beginning of the game with UNC, Werber fired a ball at Crosson's head. He ducked and the ball hit Harper flush in the face, temporarily stunning him. The big man was strangely passive the rest of the game."

The actual douche bag was invented in 1848 but we're pretty sure this incident is the first time a human acted like one.

Flash forward to February 4, 1961. The incident known as "The Fight" also involves a game with North Carolina. After UNC's Larry Brown is fouled unnecessarily hard by Duke's Art Heyman, Brown takes offense and suddenly punches are being wildly thrown. A near riot follows as the UNC bench clears and Duke fans join the mob.

Notice something there? Seems to us that the Duke guy was the instigator. And, yes, this is the same Larry Brown who has since gone on to coach in the ABA as well as every team in the NBA. Twice.

Next up is a matchup in the Coach K era that will be forever known as "The Bloody Montross Game." Duke is coming off a national title and rolls into Chapel Hill on February 5, 1992, as the number one team in the country. During a hard-fought game battling down low, UNC center Eric Montross gets bashed and a gigantic cut opens on his noggin. He steps to the foul line toward

Pieces of Laettner's elbow still show up in Eric Montross's X-ray.
(Courtesy of Scott Williams)

7

the end of the game with blood running down his cheek and the side of his head. Carolina ultimately wins the game 75–73.

Montross says that he still gets asked about that game more than any other. We attended that game and will admit that maybe a few tears of joy were shed in the stands. And later that night, a mob formed on Franklin Street, and Montross came strolling down the street, a fresh bandage under his left eye.

Not even two months later in March 1992, came the infamous Christian Laettner "Stomp." No blood, but still dirty.

When you get to 2003 and talk about Dahntay (or should we say "Dirtay") Jones, how can you pick one incident? Let's see, there's January 12, 2003, when he broke Wake Forest freshman Justin Gray's jaw setting a screen. Then roughly two months later, he swung an elbow and cut UNC freshman Raymond Felton on the chin. (No foul was called on that, by the way.) That ruckus led to a heated exchange between then-coach Matt Doherty and Duke assistant coach Chris Collins that almost caused punches to be thrown.

And "Dirtay" didn't clean up once he got to the pros. Any Phoenix Suns fans out there? Then you'll remember May 2, 2005, when he nearly tackled Shawn Marion during a transition layup attempt in the playoffs. Marion's teammate Quentin Richardson told the *Arizona Republic* after the game, "I didn't like it. If we were somewhere else, there would've been a fight. If this were the regular season, [Jones] would've been in the front row. He would've been somewhere, and I would've been on top of him. That [stuff] is unnecessary, and it's not basketball."

In 2009, Jones was nearly suspended from the NBA playoffs after a flagrant foul on Kobe Bryant—his third flagrant of the postseason and his second in two games. Lakers coach Phil Jackson accused Jones of "unacceptable defense, tripping guys, and playing unsportsmanlike basketball."

On February 20, 2005, Duke was coming off a two-game losing streak when they hosted the Wake Forest Demon Deacons for a Top 20 battle. Coach K mysteriously shook up the starting lineup and put in little-used reserve Patrick Davidson. His orders? Basically to harass the bejeezus out of star Deacon guard, Chris Paul.

"He manhandled Wake Forest guard Chris Paul on the opening possession, bumping him wildly before a foul was called," the Associated Press wrote. "He left the game after two minutes to a rousing ovation and got a warm embrace from Blue Devils coach Mike Krzyzewski."

Patrick finished the game with a stat line of two minutes played, two personal fouls, thirteen slaps on the ass from his teammates, and one creepy hug. Oh, and after the season he added something else: the Coach's Award, Duke's trophy for the person who personifies the team's values.

Not that dirty play always involves blood. Consider this priceless anecdote from UNC guard Bobby Frasor.

Years ago as an eighth grader, Frasor was attending a basketball summer camp.

"Before camp would start all the campers would play. And in 8th grade I was pretty good so I played with some of the older guys," he says. "We were playing against [current Duke assistant coaches] Chris Collins and Steve Wojciechowski. And I'm tying my shoe getting ready to play and Wojo throws it into Collins and he goes up for a layup. At the time I didn't think about, but looking back on it, well, that's Duke."

Damn straight.

Verdict: What have we got? A stunned center, a near riot, a bleeding face during a free throw, a foot to the chest of a man lying on the ground, a broken jaw, a cut chin, pissed-off pros, two fouls and a creepy hug, a cheap play, and the bloody nose to end all bloody noses. That's enough evidence to keep CSI forensic investigators busy for years.

CHARGE #2

THE ANNOYING, POINTLESS FLOOR SLAP.

Duke may not have invented the floor slap—that useless, horribly juvenile gesture in which the players hunker down way low and smack the court to show everyone that they mean business—but, like the CIA with waterboarding, they sure as hell did it most annoyingly.

If only the floor could slap back.

No one's quite sure who invented the gesture, but what is certain is that it was brought to Duke by Coach K during his initial season in 1980. It was road-tested by that first team that included Gene Banks, Kenny Dennard, and Vince Taylor. Two years later, it was adopted by Jay Bilas, Johnny Dawkins, and the rest of the Blue Devils, who heartily pounded their way to a 3–11 conference record.

Since then, the floor slap has been deployed so many times by so many players during so many games—both important and inconsequential—that it has become a Duke signature. Ask anyone to free-associate three things that they know about Duke and this, along with lacrosse rape, will probably make the list.

"It's not like it's on page thirty-seven of a guidebook we hand everybody: When to floor-slap," assistant coach Steve Wojciechowski, told *Sports Illustrated* back in 2005.

Except that it is. The floor slap is something that Coach K actively teaches. It's behavior that is not spontaneous and organic, like instructing a child to ride a bike or teaching William Avery how to do math. It is learned, and that's why it's so damn annoying.

The move grew out of something Coach K taught in practice, and he occasionally signaled from the bench during games that he wanted his boys to bend over and smack away.

"It was K's way of showing us that if we did what he said we would own the defensive floor, that no one would get by us," Mark Alarie said in *Tales from the Duke Blue Devils Hardwood*.

No one would argue that emotion isn't a part of basketball. During the heat of the game, plenty of things happen spontaneously. Players pump their fists, they shout, they pat their teammate's ass inappropriately. All good.

But Duke's floor slap has become so calculated, such a vain, look-at-me gesture that it long ago ceased to have any meaning. You do anything enough times—be it fly to the moon, have sex with Kim Kardashian, or slap Coach K's court—and it's bound to become less special.

In his book *Blue Blood: Duke-Carolina: Inside the Most Storied Rivalry in College Hoops*, Art Chansky reports that during the 1988 season, Coach K actually had to order his players to rein in the endless floor slapping. "They would just do it and play our regular defense," Coach K said. Instead of "regular" defense, Coach K then barked that his team should start playing some "fucking defense." Whether that brand requires floor slapping is unclear.

What is clear: The floor slap is just plain stupid. It's beyond meaningless. It should be outlawed, and violators should be punished by having to actually drive a nonluxury automobile.

The floor slap is one of those things that is pounded into the head of every Duke player until it becomes habitual, unquestioned behavior. It's no different from a brainwashed cult member wearing purple Nikes or shaving his head and shaking a tambourine at a bus station.

Don't think so? Just ask Jamal Boykin.

The forward, who played at Duke from 2005 to 2007, was so eager to gain admission into the cult of Duke and all its required behaviors that he completely drank the floor-slapping Kool-Aid.

He is probably the first dumb-ass in the history of the world to slap the floor during the 2006 annual Blue-White game. Yes, during a scrimmage. Against his own team. That's sort of like making a throat-slitting gesture after you've just blocked the shot of the fat kid from *Modern Family* during a celebrity charity game.

A few weeks later, Boykin again got so fired up that he broke out the floor slap during the first game of his career. Only problem was, Duke was up by 40 points on lowly Columbia at the time. (The Blue Devils went on to win 86–43.)

"It was to the point that it was disrespectful to the other team," Boykin later said.

Ya think?

And the most embarrassing part of it all was that Boykin was hardly a difference maker. This was not a baller who was putting up double-doubles and carrying the team. Boykin scored four points in that Columbia game, which wound up being his only points of the entire season. He transferred to Cal a year later.

When the Bulls' Michael Jordan talks trash, you humbly accept it and ask for more, if-you-would-be-so-kind, sir. When the Bulls' Will Perdue does it, you almost feel sorry for the guy.

And it's not like the floor slap is always an effective, cohesive force for good. It can sometimes backfire, as it did in a big way back in 2008 when West Virginia met the Blue Devils in the second round of the NCAA tournament.

Duke got manhandled by the Mountaineers 73–67, marking the team's second straight pre–Sweet Sixteen flameout. Toward the end of the game, WVA guard Joe Mazzulla, who had thirteen points, eleven rebounds, and eight assists, threw Duke's tradition right back in their face and mockingly smacked the floor.

Teammate Joe Alexander would later tell Yahoo! Sports, "Man, Joe Mazzulla slapping the floor—that was just such a great thing to happen in my life."

You don't suppose that Mazzulla and the rest of the team took Duke's floor-slapping tradition as a personal slap in their face? You don't suppose they used it as motivation, do you?

There's a reason not a single other college program has a similar tradition. Slapping the floor is pathetic. It's nothing more than a taunt from a team too elitist to talk trash. Real teams speak with their game, not with their clownish gestures.

Verdict: Guilty. Time to leave the damn floor alone.

EXHIBIT A

GRADUATION RATES

D on't you love hearing announcers prattle on about how Duke is a bastion of academic prowess and how its players personify the term *student-athlete*? Judge for yourself. Here's a list of the Atlantic Coast Conference's graduation success rates for hoops players in 2010, as determined by the National Collegiate Athletic Association (NCAA).

Wake Forest 100%
Boston College 88%
North Carolina 88%
Duke 83%
Virginia Tech 75%
Florida State 73%
Miami 73%
Clemson 71%
North Carolina State 60%
Virginia 35%
Georgia Tech 36%
Maryland 31%

CHARGE #3

THE ONLY WAY THE TOURNAMENT SELECTION COMMITTEE COULD GIVE DUKE AN EASIER ROAD TO THE FINAL FOUR EVERY YEAR WOULD BE TO DRAW THEM A MAP.

For the Blue Devils, Christmas comes in March every year.

Can't you just picture the team gathering round a roaring fire in Krzyzewski's dungeon, lil' Wojo bouncing on the coach's knee, to watch the tournament-selection show.

"I could barely sleep last night!" squeals assistant coach Chris Collins, still inexplicably in his pajamas, even though it's 7 P.M.

"I dreamed of sugar plum fairies! And playing a weak number-four seed in the Sweet Sixteen who has lost its only consequential player to injury!" chimes in Nate James.

Suddenly, a hush falls across the room. Somewhere a clock bongs. Coach K pauses, takes a sip of his patented "backache juice" (it's gin and baby-seal's blood, if you must know), touches the tip of his nose twice, and then . . .

And then . . .

And then something miraculous happens. A blinding flash of light erupts from the magic television box. A great wind blows from the mouth of ESPN's Dickie V (or Dick Vitale). Beautiful theme music fills the air, and the little elves on the selection committee drop another beautifully wrapped present down Duke's chimney. And as always, it's more than anyone in Durham could have hoped for.

Like we said: Christmas in March.

For years, basketball fans have grumbled about the seeming preferential treatment the Blue Devils get come tournament time. It's almost like the selection committee gift-wraps a pleasant stroll to the Final Four just for them. Germany met more resistance rolling into Poland.

With each unveiling of the annual bracket, every number one seed Duke is handed (which, let's face it, is pretty much always), the doubters keep coming. And rarely more so than in 2010, where Duke was set up as a number one seed in what was considered the weakest region, the South, despite being a border-line contender for the top line in the first place. Villanova, the bracket's number two, was viewed as the least formidable of second seeds (the team went on to fold in the second round), while the number four, Purdue, was without its best player, Robbie Hummel, who had torn his ACL a few weeks earlier. The Blue Devils ultimately sashayed to Indianapolis to beat Butler (a number five seed) for the championship.

The pretournament chatter, as usual, was all about the present the selection committee had once again left under Duke's tree.

"Given the world's penchant for believing Duke gets prefer-ential treatment every year," wrote ESPN's Tim Keown, "wouldn't you think the committee would go out of its way to make sure it doesn't happen—just once?"

Not that year.

Even *Sports Illustrated*'s Seth Davis, a Duke alum, couldn't believe his eyes. He questioned the wisdom of seeding Duke ahead of both West Virginia and Syracuse—the latter having won the regular-season title in a tougher conference and finished the year with one fewer loss than Duke.

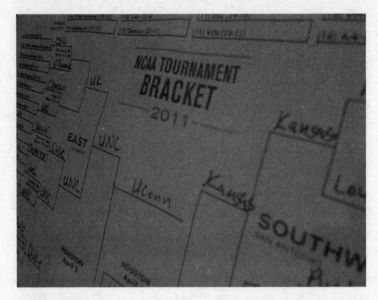

Which Division III girl's school will Duke meet in the tourney this year?

The pro-Duke conspiracy sentiment became so widespread that Coach K was asked about it at a press conference the day before the team's first tourney game.

"As a coach, I don't pay any attention to that," he said. "If I was a fan, I think I'd pay a lot of attention because everybody talks about that. [I] don't talk about that at all because it has no bearing on our performance."

Yet, second-guessing Duke's charitable tourney journey has become as much a part of the tournament's fabric as "One Shining Moment." In 2007, the unranked Blue Devils scored a number six seed after a fairly mediocre season, going .500 in the conference. Georgia Tech, who also went 8-8 in the ACC that year (and beat Duke) was a number ten. In 2011, eyebrows were raised when

Duke, as a number one seed, was paired with number two San Diego State, hardly a perennial tourney powerhouse.

"Coach [Roy] Williams had the entire team over to his house, and we had some food and watched Selection Sunday as a team," says UNC guard Daniel Bolick of 2011. "And I remember looking at our bracket and having to potentially play Washington and Syracuse as a potential matchup in the Sweet Sixteen and everything about us struggling with the zone. And then seeing Duke's selection and seeing a much, much easier road than some of the other number one seeds, and they were supposed to be the fourth number one seed, meaning they should have had the hardest draw of all the number one seeds. I started thinking, 'You gotta be kidding me, this is ridiculous.'"

No one's claiming tournament seeding is an exact science, but something must be going on for the team to be on the wrong end of so many complaints over the years.

"Favoritism? I just don't see it," says ESPN bracketologist Joe Lunardi. "I don't think there is a factual basis for the easier-path argument, and I believe that there are too many safeguards in place within the committee's principles and procedures for intentional straying to take place."

Generally, grumbles about the Dookies and their tournament waltz come in three areas: Duke always seems to play close to home, they are given a higher seed than they deserve, and they are always slotted into the easiest bracket.

First, the question of geographical favoritism.

"Duke typically plays close to home for the first two rounds, yes, but usually their résumé merits a high seed that warrants that kind of preferred placement," says David Mihm, editor and founder of bracketography.com. "The same thing often happens with Kansas, Kentucky, UCLA, Connecticut, and other blue bloods who consistently earn high seeds, so to single Duke out for that kind of treatment seems a bit unfair."

Year after year, Duke often has an arena to play in close to home, because the ACC has been very successful at winning bids to host tourney games, Lunardi says.

Now for the overseeding charge.

"This is probably the most common argument that I hear from disgruntled fans," Mihm admits. "The only time it's really stood out as a glaring error in judgment by the committee in recent memory was 2010 when Duke received a higher seed than a very good Syracuse team, presumably because they won the ACC Tournament and Syracuse didn't win the Big East tournament. They might have been overseeded as a number six seed in 2007, but that was not a very good team and I don't think many people expected them to make a deep run no matter where they were placed. The fact is that most years, the committee seems to seed Duke appropriately based on its résumé."

Finally, the "easy bracket" argument. To believe that Duke is intentionally handed a cake walk to the Final Four, you'd have to believe there's willful corruption going on within the committee.

"I haven't seen one spit of evidence to suggest it," Lunardi says. "There's so much scrutiny now of the committee. In the old days, the nontransparency days, a [former NCAA director] Walter Byers smoke-filled room, I can't say if there was or wasn't horse trading, but there was at least a way for it to occur and nobody to really care or notice. Well, those days are gone."

"Frankly, it's way too hard most years for the committee to seed the bracket in accordance with seeding principles of geographic balance, avoiding conference conflicts and regular season rematches to think about who has the easiest road relative to other seeds on the same line," Mihm says. "There are always curious decisions every year, but I don't think the committee systematically favors Duke or goes out of its way to set up marquee games for them."

And why would they? What would anyone gain by favoring Duke? Well, money for one.

According to Nielsen in 2010, North Carolina's triangle (home to Durham) is the second biggest college basketball TV market in the country, behind Louisville, and Duke consistently earns bigger TV ratings than other college teams. (Don't get too excited, Dookies. As one CBS exec explained, many viewers are tuning in because they're hoping to see Duke lose. Source for the CBS exec quote is: http://www.mndaily.com/2010/03/31/ncaa-tourney -sees-increase-elite-eight-tv-ratings.) One popular theory making the rounds in 2010 was that the NCAA would like nothing more than for Duke to make it as far as possible, because of the eyeballs the teams draws.

"Recently, ratings for the tournament have not exactly been off the charts," wrote the *New York Daily News* in 2010, before Duke cake-walked to a title. "The NCAA need to reverse this trend—now. The selection committee knew the NCAA is in the process of deciding whether to opt out of the final three years (2011–13) of its eleven-year, $6 billion contract with CBS. If the contract is put on the open market, it is smart [TV] business to attempt to maximize—big-time—the 2010 tourney's ratings."

"Are we saying then that the NCAA fixes games?" Lunardi

asks. "This is like the argument that the NBA wants the Lakers and the Celtics in the finals. I just don't have any evidence to support it. It just doesn't seem that the marquee markets win at a disproportionate enough rate in any sport to justify the argument that scripting is going on."

Fair enough. It might be difficult to believe that the fix is completely in, but it's easier to accept that the committee members are human beings, and like the rest of us, they aren't immune to the power of brands. If it comes down to giving the benefit of the doubt to a lesser-known mid-major or a blue-chip brand like Kentucky, North Carolina, or, yes, Duke, which way do you think the committee will consciously or subconsciously lean?

And Christmas will come early to Durham yet again.

Verdict: We can't quite absolve the Blue Devils of all charges, but this might be the one conspiracy theory that's overblown.

CHARGE #4

THEIR MASCOT IS INCREDIBLY LAME. AND WORSE, FRENCH.

Just look at him. He has a pudgy face and shoulder pads. He carries a large fork and sometimes wears headbands emblazoned with wacky sayings, like END OF THE RHODE when Duke faced Rhode Island. Or how about ALL UCONN EAT: FRIED HUSK-PUPPIES during the 2004 Final Four game against Connecticut? Freaking hilarious. And let's not forget February 7, 1988, when a black Notre Dame player, David Rivers, was treated to a headband that read BUCKWHEAT.

Duke classmates question what that stick thing in the mascot's hand is, having never seen one before. *(Courtesy of Rob Goodlatte)*

Or was that printed on the white pointed hood the acne-covered nerd in a costume wore on his head to proudly represent DuKKKe University that day?

Look, we know mascots aren't easy. We know every third sports team in America is called the Tigers. We realize a Tar Heel is basically a dirty foot. We know a Terrapin is an animal that lives in a shell and can move fifteen feet in two hours. (But, hey, at least it can snap.) We know that if someone says they cheer for the Wildcats, you not only have to narrow it down to the state but maybe even to the USPS-verified Zip+4 spot on a map to figure out who they're talking about.

So when in September 1921, Duke's student newspaper launched a campaign to pick a "catchy name, one of our own possession that would be instantly recognizable nationwide in songs, yells and publicity," the hunt for a mascot could have gone in many directions. Reportedly, "Captains," "Dreadnaughts," and "Royal Blazes" were all in play. We're pretty sure a member of the cat family was a choice somewhere along the line.

But someone slapped "Blue Devils" on the list, and it reluctantly stuck.

Go ahead and savor the irony of the newspaper's editors picking the epitome of evil to represent a Methodist university. Or of their prescience in choosing a representation of Lucifer at a school that would come to be known as pure evil some sixty years later.

As it turns out, though, the mascot choice had little to do with religious symbols.

According to the Duke University archives, the Blue Devil mascot was named after—my God, are you going to love this—a French military unit. That's right, the same crack armed forces that are now a punch line for surrendering at the first pop of a firecracker.

The story goes that *"Les Diables Bleus"* was the nickname for a group of French soldiers in World War I called the Chasseurs Alpins. They were well known because of their "flowing cape and jaunty berets."

Allow us to repeat that. Jaunty. Berets.

Do you think that when Dahntay Jones so proudly tore his Blue Devil uniform from his chest in triumph that he had any idea he was actually hearkening back to some snail-eater running around the Alps in a spiffy hat that hung off the side of his head?

And let's not forget about the cape. Oooooooo, a cape! I'm so freaking scared. Mascots are supposed to strike fear into their opponent's heart, not provide a little warmth when it gets breezy.

Somewhere along the lines, Duke ditched the idea of the militaristic theme and went straight to a more classic devil with horns. And what says "menacing" more than a head topper that looks like an overcooked muffin fresh out of the oven? Maybe it would have been better, however, for Duke to go back to the traditional looking getup instead of dressing a guy in a big clunky devil suit. Maybe a cape would have helped the poor bastard inside the devil suit who, in February 2008, jumped about a foot off the ground during a time-out in a basketball game and promptly twisted his ankle.

Okay, fine. So what if Duke had no idea what they were doing in the 1920s when they settled on Monsieur Capey. But maybe there is more to this that isn't being revealed. Maybe there are things we don't know about the Chasseurs Alpins that actually make them the perfect choice for the Duke mascot. Maybe these flowy-caped, beret-wearing boys—as they retreated to defend their home turf—put their rifles aside just for a second to slap their palms on the battlefield. Maybe they always lost their battles because they stuck to a rigid seven-soldier rotation and didn't get anything from the guys sitting on their asses back at camp. Maybe they brought in the best soldiers from all over the country year after year, only to see them transfer to another country because they were originally told they would get to be a shooting guard instead of setting screens for the real soldiers.

But there is one thing for sure that the French soldiers did just like Greg Paulus, Shane Battier, and Wojo. When the enemy got close, they flopped.

Verdict: As the French would say, *"Coupable!"*

EXHIBIT B

TOP 5 DUKE SCANDALS

5. PERENNIAL TOURNAMENT CHOKER J. J. REDICK BLOWS SOMETHING ELSE: A .11 BLOOD ALCOHOL LEVEL

The Duke guard was pulled over in June 2006 after he made an illegal U-turn in order to avoid a drunk-driving checkpoint near the Duke campus. The arresting officer noted that Redick had "very glassy eyes, strong odor of alcohol coming from breath." He eventually pleaded guilty and received one year's probation,

Redick in his mug shot, rocking a half-popped collar and fully glazed eyes. *(Courtesy of the Durham County Sheriff's Office)*

as well as twenty-four hours of community service. His license was suspended for sixty days.

4. THE CHEAT IS ON

In 1995, center Greg Newton—who's less known for his prowess on the court than for stupidly calling Tim Duncan "soft" and "babyish"—was suspended from school for two semesters after he was found guilty of cheating on an exam. In 1997, Ricky Price received a two-semester suspension because of academic problems. He was reportedly booted for plagiarism. Both players were welcomed back to the team. "These things happen to students, and he's one," Coach K said of Price at the time. "We're fully committed to him."

3. THIS LITTLE PIGGIE GOES TO PRISON

In 2000, former Duke star Corey Maggette admitted that while still in high school, he had illegally accepted $2,000 from his summer-league coach—a man with the unfortunate name of Myron Piggie. A year later, the coach was sentenced to thirty-seven months in prison for fraud. Maggette left Duke for the NBA after his freshman year, and while the NCAA could have stripped the school of its wins for the 1999 season and its Final Four banner, no action was taken. The NCAA's lengthy investigation ultimately determined that Maggette and Duke were unaware of the payments. Try and make sense of that.

2. WILL WORK FOR FOOD. AND JEEP CHEROKEES.

On the list of shady things that went down at Duke, perhaps the shadiest involves jobs secured by players' parents—often under mysterious circumstances. Chris Duhon's mother, Vivian Harper, moved from Louisiana to Durham when her son enrolled at Duke in 2000, and perhaps not coincidentally, landed a job at a financial company owned by a Duke booster who kept a signed 1991 championship ball on his desk. She was reportedly under-qualified and overpaid for the job. In Louisiana, her house was nearly foreclosed on and she drove a 1972 VW Beetle. Once she landed in Durham, a Jeep Cherokee and Nissan Altima were registered in her name. Carlos Boozer's father, Carlos Sr., also seemed to benefit from his son enrolling at Duke. In 2000, he moved his family from Alaska to Durham, and three months after arriving, he was given a nice gig at GlaxoSmithKline as an administrative assistant. The firm's boss, Robert Ingram, was a close friend of Krzyzewski's. Boozer left the company six months after his son declared for the NBA draft.

1. PETE GAUDET GETS THROWN UNDER THE BUS
So much for loyalty. The 1994–95 season was infamous, not only because of how terrible the usually solid Blue Devils were, but because it may represent one of the lowest things done to one coach by another. Pete Gaudet had been Coach K's assistant for more than a decade, and when K took a leave from the program in January 1995 because of exhaustion and back problems, Gaudet became interim head coach. When he took over, the team was a respectable 9-3 and ranked number seven in the nation. From there, though, things went downhill, and the Devils ended up finishing 4-14 and missing the NCAA tournament. Duke later petitioned the NCAA to have those losses hung on Gaudet, K's loyal assistant and a man who was making just $16,000 a year, according to the *New York Times*.

What really rankles haters is the suspicion that Krzyzewski

may have bailed on the season because he knew his team was going to be subpar, and he saw Gaudet as a convenient scapegoat. K didn't bow out until after the first ACC game of the season, an embarrassing beatdown at the hands of Clemson, who hadn't previously won at Cameron since 1984. With a lineup that included three freshmen, the coach probably knew things weren't going to get better. He pulled the plug to have back surgery, and at the time, the university announced he'd be back in a few weeks. As Duke continued going winless in the conference, K announced he would be sitting out the entire season.

During this time, however, he was still plenty healthy enough to receive recruits, including a highly touted forward out of Florida named Vince Carter. "He was up and about," Carter told *Sports Illustrated* at the time. "He didn't seem like a guy who has had all these back problems. He's just anxious to get back. He misses his players."

Coach K eventually returned after the season concluded and those around him say he was a different person: angrier, more focused. He promptly called his assistant coaches into a meeting and chewed them out royally, telling them only he was irreplaceable and that they sullied Duke's impeccable standards.

Gaudet, not surprisingly, did not return to the program the next season. Two other assistants also left or quit.

"I think I should have been credited with all the losses," Krzyzewski admitted in a 2007 press conference. "Overall, the bottom line is I'm responsible even though I'm not there. That's the way I looked at it, but it doesn't make any difference to me. I wouldn't want the wins, let's put it that way. But you can give me the losses." Anyone gonna take him up on that?

CHARGE #5

THE WORD "LIFETIME" EVIDENTLY DOESN'T MEAN THE SAME THING TO COACH K AS IT DOES TO THE REST OF US.

Let's say you're unhappy in your job. You feel underappreciated, you don't think you're earning nearly enough bread, and man, what's a worker bee gotta do to get another week of vacation around here? If you're a regular schlub, working at Burger King or an accounting firm, you're pretty much out of luck when it comes to negotiating. Go ahead and march into your boss's office to demand that your salary be doubled and that you be given a chauffeur-driven ride to the office each day and see how quickly the door bangs you in the ass on the way out.

Too bad you can't threaten to defect to the NBA.

Hey, it worked for Coach K.

The Duke skipper has contemplated leaving for the pros a few times during his career. Fair enough. There are as many high-profile college coaches who have thought about bolting for the NBA as there are zeroes in the average Duke student's bank account balance.

But the difference between most coaches and Krzyzewski is that Coach K has wrestled with these offers very publicly, causing much hand-wringing among his players, the Duke admin, and whoever is being paid millions to dye his hair.

He has also been rewarded spectacularly for staying put.

Exhibit A: Coach K's most famous flirtation with the NBA,

an excruciating (for Duke fans, anyway) courtship with the Los Angeles Lakers in 2004.

In an especially classy touch, the news of the coach's potential defection broke on Duke president Richard Brodhead's first day in office.

"Welcome to Duke, Richard," Coach K seemed to be saying. "Now lemme show you who's actually in charge around here."

Brodhead was left to settle in at his new job by desperately picking up a bullhorn, gathering some students, and embarrassing himself by leading an impromptu pep rally outside Cameron to try and persuade Coach K to stay.

But it was not cheering that the coach was apparently after.

After Duke announced that Krzyzewski had been talking with the Lakers (the school curiously said it was releasing the news to be "proactive instead of reactive"), Duke's senior vice president for public and government relations John Burness declared that "it's reasonable to assume some modifications will be made" to the coach's contract.

Only it wasn't exactly "reasonable."

The problem was, Coach K had just three years earlier signed a "lifetime" contract with the university that was intended to keep him there for the rest of his career. It was a lifetime contract—as in, the only way out was in a pine box.

When he signed the pact, K proclaimed his love of the university and committed to being a part of Duke for good, in spite of the occasional offers from NBA teams.

"I wish [reporters would] start asking a pro coach, 'Are you going college?'" Krzyzewski said at a 2001 press conference announcing the deal. "To me, I got the better job, at least for me."

Well, that didn't last long. Three years later, Duke athletics director Joe Alleva was admitting he'd be "able to do a few things for Mike in his contract."

According to the Associated Press, K's total compensation for the year before his brief Lakers romance was $875,048. And that's just his Duke salary, not including money from ads, speaking engagements, and shoe companies. However, that salary marked a decrease of 33 percent from the previous year when Coach K raked in $1.3 million from Duke.

Was now a good time to renegotiate?

"He has [Brodhead's] attention now like no other time," former Duke coach Bucky Waters told Greenboro's *News & Record* in 2004. "It's a great negotiating position. If Mike has some issues with his program, this is the time to deal with them. Not six months from now."

Meanwhile, Krzyzewski certainly did his part to sow doubt about his intentions during the two-week period he was contemplating the offer. According to ESPN, he walked into a gym and,

Coach K made more than $4 million for the 2010–11 season—more than the average NBA coach. *(Courtesy of Rob Goodlatte)*

to the horror of the Duke basketball personnel gathered, casually mentioned, "You'll never guess who called. Kobe Bryant. He wants me to come coach him." Nice mind game, that.

The school also increased the coach's leverage by portraying him as waffling.

"I don't think Mike knows what's going to happen right now," Duke senior associate athletics director Chris Kennedy said during that period. He then noted that Krzyzewski was "in seclusion," needing "time and distance" to make his agonizing decision.

But he wasn't in such seclusion that he couldn't take a dinner meeting with Duke's president. Among the issues that K was apparently unhappy about were his team's basketball digs.

"He'd like to have a practice facility," Kennedy admitted. "We'd like to have a practice facility to relieve pressure on our other facilities."

Once K eventually announced he was returning to Duke, that practice facility became a reality. Ground was broken in September 2006 on the $15.2-million Michael W. Krzyzewski Center for Academic & Athletic Excellence, a massive 56,000-square-foot building adjacent to Cameron that housed two full-size basketball courts on which the team could practice flopping.

Was Krzyzewski ever serious about coaching the Lakers, or was this just some hardball negotiating tactic with the university that had recently handed him a generous lifetime contract?

A similarly suspicious storyline had played out a decade earlier. Only then, it was the Portland Trailblazers and the Miami Heat who had come calling. And as always, Coach K at least appeared to take the offers seriously.

The prospect of losing their coach (and one of their most effective fund-raisers) caused the Duke honchos to do a spit-take with their Chablis and spring into action. Then-president Nan Keohane cut her vacation short and returned to Durham over Memorial Day to meet with Krzyzewski and to address whatever grievances he had. Among them were reportedly the administration's failure to install air-conditioning in rickety old Cameron—an improvement that had been discussed for years. K was also angling for an addition to the arena that would include new locker rooms, offices, a hall of fame, and a crypt into which to toss Pete Gaudet.

Anyway, you can see where this is going. The new Schwartz-Butters Athletic Center opened at the end of the 1997–98 season. It followed an upgrade that gave Cameron a new state-of-the-art floor in 1996, which would be later named Coach K Court in November 2000. A $3-million air-conditioning system was finally added in 2002.

Were these straight quid pro quo situations, where Krzyzewski would threaten to leave every time he wanted a building or salary upgrade, like a toddler holding her breath until she's given a lollipop? You'd probably never be able to conclusively prove it, but as Coach K suggests in his book on motivation, follow your heart and see what it tells you.

And now a couple of postscript points. Lost in all the Lakers drama was the fact that L.A.'s general manager Mitch Kupchak had offered the job to UNC's Roy Williams before Coach K. You didn't read much about that. And unlike his counterpart at Duke, Williams turned the job down flat as opposed to launching an episode of *As the Basketball Turns,* which played out in every newspaper and on every sports radio show across the country.

"Coach Smith wanted to get it out in the media that the Lakers had offered the job to me before they offered it to Duke's coach

Mike Krzyzewski," Williams wrote in *Hard Work: A Life On and Off the Court*. "I said, 'Coach, that's not important.'"

Guess he didn't need a new locker room.

As for Coach K, his days of earning a paltry $875,000 are long gone. He pulled in $4,195,519 during the 2010–11 season, making him the second-highest-paid college basketball coach to Louisville's Rick Pitino, according to *USA Today*.

Verdict: Guilty as hell. K's behavior is especially galling considering the comments he has made over the years about some of his players who made the jump to the NBA and bailed on the Duke family.

CHARGE #6

DUKE IS WHERE BIG MEN'S CAREERS GO TO DIE.

Quick, name a Duke post player since 1998 that has averaged fifteen or more points for their career. And we're not talking about the taller guys that drift out to the perimeter to jack threes, like Skeletor and McLovin. (You may know them by their Christian names, Kyle Singler and Ryan Kelly.)

Need a refresher? Here's a list of Dookies who were all ranked in the Top 100 coming out of high school: Carlos Boozer, Casey Sanders, Shelden Williams, Shavlik Randolph, Michael Thompson, David McClure, Josh McRoberts, Eric Boateng, Lance Thomas, Brian Zoubek, Miles and Mason Plumlee, and Josh Hairston.

Don't be blinded by Boozer's alarming amount of chest hair; he didn't crack fifteen points. No, it's not the man whose eyes are set so far apart that he looks like Admiral Akbar from *Star Wars* ("It's a trap!"), Shelden Williams, either.

Actually, it's none of them. Not a single one.

Hell, only three of them even averaged double figures. Contrast that with the coach of their biggest rival, Roy Williams, who has coached eight post players since 1998 that have averaged double-digit points per game. Including Sean May, who averaged sixteen and Tyler Hansbrough, who averaged twenty.

If you watch Duke play on a regular basis, these stats don't surprise you. A big man in a Blue Devil uniform gets all the respect of a lowly untouchable in India, whose job is to shut his leprosied mouth and sweep the path for the chosen ones—in Duke's case, the three-point shooters. Set screens, shag rebounds, and rub Kyle Singler's feet. This is the plight of a big man at Duke. Were the team to run three set plays in a single game for a particular post player, someone would have to call Guinness.

It would be easy to blame Wojo, who is their designated big man coach. No, really, he is. All five-foot-something of him. That little Oompa Loompa must be too busy fishing the corpse of Augustus Gloop out of the chocolate river to teach anyone a jump hook.

But let's go beyond Points Per Game. Way beyond. Let's put together a comparison of post players ranked in the Top 100 coming out of high school that have been coached by Roy Williams and Coach K since 1998. We wanted to examine two things: (1) How have they developed during their tenure at their respective schools? (2) Did their time at UNC or Duke help or hurt their prospects for being drafted by an NBA team?

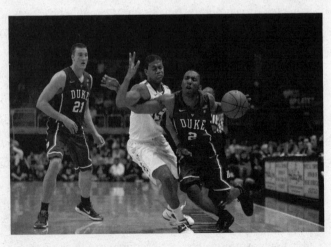

Duke big men: more useless than a human appendix. *(Courtesy of Luis Blanco, Press Photographer)*

First, a look at their development:

	COACH K's BIGS[1]	ROY'S BIGS[2]
Actual Offensive Rating	106.1	109.6
Expected Offensive Rating	105.4	106.3
Deviation from Expectation	+0.7%	+3.1%
Actual % Possessions Used	17.7	22.8
Expected % Possessions Used	22.2	22.5
Deviation from Expectation	−20.0%	+1.4%
Actual Season-to-Season Improvement[3]	98.5	111.2
Expected Season-to-Season Improvement	109.3	110.2
Deviation from Expectation	−9.9%	+0.9%

1. This sample includes fourteen players: Carlos Boozer (RSCI rank #8), Casey Sanders (#16), Shelden Williams (#8), Shavlik Randolph (#14), Michael Thompson (#30), David McClure (#71), Josh McRoberts (#1), Eric Boateng (#39), Jamal Boykin (#60), Lance Thomas (#20), Brian Zoubek (#25), Miles Plumlee (#81), Mason Plumlee (#18), and Josh Hairston (#32). These players combine for thirty-seven player-seasons and twenty-three season-to-season (e.g., freshman-to-sophomore) development periods.

2. This sample includes twelve players: Drew Gooden (#21), Nick Collison (#22), Wayne Simien (first two seasons only—#20), Sean May (final two seasons only—#9), Tyler Hansbrough (#4), Brandan Wright (#3), Deon Thompson (#43), Alex Stepheson (#39), Ed Davis (#9), Tyler Zeller (#18), Travis Wear (#38), and John Henson (#5). These players combine for thirty player-seasons and nineteen season-to-season development periods.

3. Indexed such that 100 represents no season-to-season improvement and 110 represents a 10% season-to-season improvement. Numbers less than 100 indicate that a player actually regressed from one season to the next (a 90, for example, means that a player is 10 percent worse in the second of consecutive seasons).

(Stats compiled by Adrian Atkinson.)

What immediately jumps out at you is that percent of possessions. The stats confirm what your eyes tell you when you are watching. Duke lets its big men molder in the post like old cheese. In fact, they get 20 percent fewer possessions than expected and more than 20 percent fewer possessions than Roy-coached bigs.

But the most damning thing in this first table is that since 1998, the average Duke big man has actually *regressed* by 10 percent by going to Duke. Now, Roy's players aren't dramatically improving, but at least they are moving in the right direction. What's that saying about a ship that sits in the harbor will eventually have a rusty hull?

Read that again, high school basketball players: IF YOU GO TO DUKE, YOU WILL GET WORSE. The numbers don't lie. And to think that Duke was still able to recruit three straight Plumlee brothers. Fail.

So, what happens to these same players when they move on from Duke and enter the NBA? Does the Duke name bump them up the big board? In a word, *Hell No.* (Okay, that was two.)

Here's another chart for you. We call it "Expected vs. Actual NBA Draft Position for Krzyzewski and Williams Big Men in the Recruiting Services Consensus Index (RSCI) Era (1998–2011)."

	COACH K'S BIGS	ROY'S BIGS
Expected Lottery	22.6%	26.6%
Actual Lottery	9.1%	60.0%
Percentage-point Difference	−13.5%	+33.4%
Expected (non-lottery) 1st Round	13.0%	12.2%

Actual (non-lottery) 1st Round	0.0%	10.0%
Percentage-point Difference	−13.0%	−2.2%
Expected (total) 1st Round	35.6%	38.8%
Actual (total) 1st Round	9.1%	70.0%
Percentage-point Difference	−26.5%	+31.2%
Expected 2nd Round	18.2%	18.3%
Actual 2nd Round	18.2%	0.0%
Percentage-point Difference	0.0%	−18.3%
Expected Undrafted	46.2%	42.9%
Actual Undrafted	72.7%	30.0%
Percentage-point Difference	+26.5%	−12.9%
Expected Transfer	24.4%	20.5%
Actual Transfer	21.4%	16.7%
Percentage-point Difference	−3.0%	−3.8%

Ouch. In case you aren't following these staggering numbers, they are basically screaming that going to Duke will not only make you worse as a player, going there will actually hurt your chances of going high in the NBA draft or of even being drafted at all.

Since 1998 (when the composite RSCI rankings were introduced), a Krzyzewski-coached big man has a 9.1 percent chance of being drafted in the lottery (compared to a weighted average of 22.6 percent for comparably ranked post players). A Roy Williams–coached post player has a 60.0 percent chance of landing in the lottery (versus a weighted average of 26.6% for comparably ranked post players). Even worse, a K-coached big man has a 72.7 percent chance of going undrafted (compared to a national average of 46.2 percent for comparably ranked bigs). A Roy-coached post player will go undrafted just 30.0 percent of the time (as compared to a national average of 42.9 percent).

What must it feel like for those fools who are dumb enough to sign up to play in the post for Duke? Is it like buying a gold watch off a street vendor and then having it turn your wrist green? Like finishing the last bite of a meal only to find a gnarly toenail? Or maybe it's like one of those urban myths where the dude passes out in a Mexican spring-break town and wakes up the next morning to find that someone has taken one of his kidneys?

Or maybe it's a whole new level beyond. Let's call it the Duke Dupe.

Verdict: Guilty. Statistically.

CHARGE #7

DUKE CAUSES CANCER

Well, not exactly, but the university owes its very existence to something that does—namely cigarettes. Sweet, satisfying, easy-on-the-throat smokes. Ahhh!

One of the early forces behind the formation of the university was Washington Duke, a former Confederate soldier and a North Carolina resident who began cultivating tobacco in the mid-1800s—with the help of slaves, of course.

By the end of the century, Duke's business was flourishing, and the formerly dirt-poor farmer was a wealthy man and the head of a large cigarette company that he ran with his sons, Benjamin and James. Most of his product was shipped north, and a once-popular line around Durham apparently joked that Duke had killed more Yankees than Robert E. Lee. (And they're not talking about the Derek Jeter kind of Yankees.)

In 1892, Duke had the bright idea to hand over $85,000 to Trinity College, a small Methodist school then located in North Carolina's Randolph County, allowing it to move to Durham. And so the seeds—or dollars—of modern-day Duke were sown.

Washington Duke would later donate another $100,000 toward the school's endowment, but it would be his son, James B. Duke, who would be most instrumental in establishing the Duke University that we know and don't really love today.

James Buchanan Duke, who was proudly named after what historians agree was one of our country's worst presidents, is considered to be the father of Big Tobacco. He's sort of like

Chancellor Palpatine to the Empire in the *Star Wars* movies. His hobbies no doubt included reading things with a monocle and lighting cigars with hundred-dollar bills.

James Duke automated the family's once-modest cigarette factory and brought in newfangled machines that could turn out 120,000 cigarettes a day. That's a lot of air pollution.

In 1890, Duke's company merged with the four other cigarette players to produce the American Tobacco Company, a massive lung-cancer-spewing conglomerate that would ultimately control 90 percent of the market and become known colloquially as the "tobacco trust." Insert ominous music here. James Duke sat at its head and his already-great wealth soon grew to astronomical levels.

Another of James Duke's gifts to the world was the emphasis he placed on advertising and marketing. One writer at the time noted that Duke "was always willing to spend in advertising a proportion of his profits, which seemed appalling to more conservative manufacturers." In other words, you can thank him for that Joe Camel painter's cap you got free back in the '80s. One of Duke's more successful marketing schemes—remember, this is a man who eventually founded a Methodist university and is buried in its chapel—was to distribute photos of actresses dressed in acrobatic tights, burlesque outfits, or other risqué costumes with his smokes. The practice rankled some of the clergy at the time.

And in an especially delicious twist, James Duke, like so many of the students that would ultimately attend his university, did not live in North Carolina. He was a longtime resident of New Jersey, specifically, on an estate in Somerville that boasted a ridiculous one thousand acres of lawn.

This statue of James Duke contends that the jury is still out on the dangers of smoking and that more study is needed.

But on to the university. In December 1924, James Duke created the Duke endowment, a $40-million charitable gift that was, in part, funded with 100,000 shares of the British-American Tobacco Company and 75,000 shares of R. J. Reynolds. Cigarettes are in Duke's DNA. The university was literally built on the backs of stained teeth and tarred lungs.

At the time, however, that fact hardly caused a stir. What did were the charges that James Duke was "buying" himself a university as a grand memorial to his family and name. Article Four of the document that established the Duke endowment seems to create a sticky quid pro quo situation. Were Trinity College to change its name to Duke University, it would get $6 million from James Duke. The document is cumbersomely worded, and defenders have claimed that the money would be given to Trinity even if it didn't change its name, but suspicions linger. Here's the exact wording from Article Four.

However, should the name of Trinity College, located at Durham, North Carolina, a body politic and incorporate, within three months from the date hereof (or such further time as the trustees hereof may allow) be changed to Duke University, then, in lieu of the foregoing provisions of this division "FOURTH" of this Indenture, as a memorial to his father, Washington Duke, who spent his life in Durham and whose gifts, together with those of Benjamin N. Duke, the brother of the party of the first part, and of other members of the Duke family, have so largely contributed toward making possible Trinity College at that place, he directs that the trustees shall expend of the corpus of this trust as soon as reasonably may be a sum not exceeding Six Million Dollars in expanding and extending said University, acquiring and improving such lands and erecting, removing, remodeling and equipping such buildings, according to such plans, as the trustees may adopt and approve for such purpose to the end that said Duke University may eventually include Trinity College as its undergraduate department for men, a School of Religious Training, a School for Training Teachers, a School of Chemistry, a Law School, a Co-ordinate College for Women, a School of Business Administration, a Graduate School of Arts and Sciences, a Medical School and an Engineering School, as and when funds are available.

Ignoring for a moment the fact that the founders of a supposed top university didn't understand what a run-on sentence was, the meaning of the wording here seems pretty clear. What else could be intended by that word "however" and the phrase "should the name be changed"?

Further sullying the Duke family name is the rumor—or is it an urban legend?—that the industrialist first tried to buy Princeton. He wanted to hand over his fortune to the Ivy League school (it's in New Jersey, cough, cough), but Princeton wouldn't have him. So he moved on to Trinity College to acquire the memorial he sought. School officials claim the story isn't true, but it is odd, don't you think, that Duke ultimately modeled his university's campus on Princeton.

If you can't buy 'em, copy 'em.

Verdict: The jury's still out. Duke probably doesn't cause cancer, but the school probably wishes it had a cleaner origin story, less littered with Lucky Strike butts, and more befitting the regal image it has of itself.

EXHIBIT C

J. J. REDICK'S POETRY

If J. J. Redick's jump shot ever deserts him (or deserts him more, we should say), has he got another career to fall back on? The former Dookie has talked about one day having his poetry published, so we passed along a few of J. J.'s verses to Michael Dumanis, director of the Cleveland State University Poetry Center, to see if Redick might have a future in the arts.

[selected verses by Redick]

No bandage can cover my scars
It's hard living a life behind invisible bars
Searching for the face of God
I'm only inspired by the poems of Nas

I can't see what my future has in store
but I move forth with the strength of a condor
The courage of a warrior
The commitment of an American soldier
These words describe the soundtrack to my life's song
My mind and body united like the Colors of Benneton

Dumanis says: "Mr. Redick clearly feels very passionately about his subject matter—his intense personal convictions about God, in particular—and the poems are essentially heavily rhymed diary entries in which Redick affirms his faith. They sound more

EXHIBIT C

like rap lyrics than poems, in that they rely exclusively on rhyming as many sentences together as possible to generate energy. They feel like the work of a beginner in that they are more interested in expressing the emotions of the writer in abstract, cliché-laden language than in creating an aesthetic experience for a reader through the use of concrete imagery and attention to line breaks and word choice.

"If Redick is serious about his literary pursuits, he should take a few creative writing classes. He should also begin actively reading all the contemporary poetry he can get his hands on. At this point, he's not really writing poems yet. If you're starting with no experience and only a vague sense of the rules of the game, you can't become a good basketball player, or even a competent JV basketball player, overnight. The arts are not that different."

CHARGE #8

DOOKIES ARE FAIR-WEATHER FANS WHO CANNOT BE COUNTED ON WHEN THEIR TEAMS GET DOWN.

Amid all the slobbering over the Cameron Crazies by Dick Vitale and the rest of the national media, one important point gets lost. These are not the best fans in America. These are the biggest hypocrites in America.

Sure, Dookies will support their teams. They will paint their faces, camp out for days, and have seniors make up clever chants for them—but only if that team is men's basketball, and only if they're winning.

During the 2006–2007 season, when the Devils finished a disappointing 22-11, attendance at Cameron cratered after a five-year decline. During some home games, as few as nine hundred students showed up. Kentucky's Rupp Arena has more people in line for pretzels.

"The attendance last year was pathetic in terms of fan support, and that's something we're trying to rectify this year," Duke's head line monitor Roberto Bazzani told ESPN in 2007.

So few bodies were filing into Cameron that the university actually instituted a program to encourage people to come support the team. They were practically begging the students to fill the seats.

Here's a chant for your cheer sheets, Dookies:

Let's say it all together/we're fair weather.

And God help the Duke player who dares to offend these student "fans" in any way.

Point guard Kyrie Irving declared for the NBA draft in spring 2011, ultimately becoming the first pick. Although it was a once-in-a-lifetime opportunity for a player to be chosen this high, Irving was rewarded for his success with a scathing open letter printed in the Duke student newspaper, *The Chronicle*, which suggested he was selfish and would fail at the next level.

"Don't follow in the footsteps of William Avery, you'll be warned; he made the wise decision to leave Duke after his sophomore year, and use the NBA as a stepping stone to an illustrious career in Europe," Chris Cusack sarcastically wrote. "Don't let those comparisons get you down, though, even if Avery did get the privilege of watching from the sidelines as his former college teammates celebrated a national championship.

"Plus, sticking around and winning a fifth national title for the Blue Devils is just selfish, even if you haven't ever won one yourself," the writer continued. "Think about it: Cameron is already full of national championship banners, and adding one of your own would ruin the symmetry in the rafters. Sure, you'll give up your chance to be remembered as one of Duke's all-time greatest basketball players, but I bet if you asked Christian Laettner, he would tell you that fans don't remember collegiate legacies anyway."

In 2005, forward Shavlik Randolph also received a similar outpouring of love from these so-called fans when he declared for the NBA draft.

"Your shot was useless from both the perimeter and around the basket, and you didn't have the lateral movement to defend anyone—not even my dad scrimmaging in a bagels-and-basketball

Sunday league," columnist Jason Strasser wrote in the school's student newspaper. "When you left, heads were turned but no tears were shed. People were confused why a player who struggled to log minutes in college would decide to declare for the NBA, but no one was upset that you left.

"The bottom line is that you will not be missed on this Duke basketball team."

And this is the way they treat people who are on their own team. On. Their. Own. Team. Ask yourself, can you honestly see something like this happening at any other school in the country? Aren't basketball fans supposed to be proud of their alumni who have made it to the pros? Isn't that the dream of every kid who is good enough to play college basketball?

Another school newspaper column, published in 2007, even turned against the school's dark overlord himself, Coach K. The writer called for Krzyzewski to be immediately fired . . . then rehired as Duke's athletic director. The coach, the reasoning went, had become too powerful and set in his ways to keep the basketball program moving forward.

"It has gotten to the point where no one in all of college basketball or on all of Duke's campus can tell Mike Krzyzewski he's wrong," the column read. "Coach K has created his own fiefdom, and he is judge, jury, and executioner. He is immune to criticism."

Still think Dookies are the best, most supportive, and downright coolest fans around?

Now take the case of Duke's football team, which has all the support of Hamas in an Israeli election.

Attendance at Durham's Wallace Wade Stadium has been straight-up pathetic, since . . . When was football invented again?

The university consistently ranks near the bottom of all Division I schools when it comes to attendance.

In 2005, Duke ranked ninety-sixth out of 117 teams. In 2006 and 2007, ninety-second out of 119 teams. In 2008, seventy-eighth. In 2009, seventy-eighth. In 2010, seventy-third out of 120 teams.

"There was something depressing about the football game this Saturday," *The Chronicle* lamented in 2004, "and it wasn't just the score. It was the low attendance and lack of student support for the team."

That same year, the athletic department was forced to hastily cancel a pigskin pep rally because so few students showed up. "There is nobody here," said one forlorn member of the promotions staff.

The Blue Devils often struggle to attract an average of 20,000

Duke's Wallace Wade Stadium. Population: 186. *(Courtesy of Cameron Graham)*

fans, and the stadium is frequently filled to three quarters capacity. (Compared to, say, Virginia Tech, which ran at 100 percent capacity.) In 2009, they ranked second to last in the ACC in attendance, even with the excitement over a second-year head coach, David Cutcliffe, and predictions that the team might finally stop completely sucking.

Which is not to say that there haven't been a few bright spots for the team of late.

For the home opener on September 10, 2009, Wallace Wade hosted 33,311 fans to watch the Blue Devils take on Richmond. (Duke, of course, lost.) This was the biggest turnout the university had seen since 2001.

There was only one problem: 22,000 tickets were given away for free to employees as part of a university promotion.

In 2010, the Blue Devils sold out of season tickets for the first time in at least ten years. How many exactly they sold is hard to say—Duke is private and does not release specific season ticket allotment numbers—but let's focus on the positive here. They sold out of season tickets! Someone pop the cork on a bottle of disgustingly expensive champagne that regular people couldn't afford! (This is Duke, after all.)

But again, there's one small problem. Duke was scheduled to host number one Alabama during the season, and some reports suggested the season tickets were bought by local football fans who couldn't get into that game any other way. Only booster club members were allowed to purchase single-game tickets to that particular contest. (Duke, of course, lost to 'Bama. Badly. Oh, so very, very badly, 62–13.)

The conventional wisdom was, once the Alabama game was done, the season-ticket buyers wouldn't use their seats for the rest of the season. Sure enough, a check of the Raleigh Craigslist listings the week after the Alabama pummeling found multiple listings for season-ticket packages, some for as little as fifty dollars.

It's also possible that many of the season tickets were bought, not by die-hard Duke football fans (which exist like Bigfoot exists), but by the Crimson Tide fans, who are known for traveling the country to support their team. An entire season-ticket package at Duke is about the same price as some single-game tix at Alabama. Duke officials admitted that at least six hundred season-ticket packages were purchased by 'Bama supporters, but judging by the sea of red that covered the stands that day, it was probably a lot more.

So the vicious cycle continues. Duke football continues to suck; Duke football fans continue to suck. Dookies will probably justify their meager attendance by saying that they don't go to the football games because the team isn't very good. But did it ever occur to any of them that the team might not be very good because it doesn't get any support?

Verdict: Guilty. A seventeenth-century sailor couldn't ask for fairer weather.

CHARGE #9

[THIS CHARGE HAS BEEN REDACTED
FOR FEAR THAT COACH K MIGHT
CALL US AND SCORCH THE
EARTH WITH F-BOMBS FOR
TWENTY MINUTES.]

There's really no way to sugarcoat this for sensitive palates, so we're just going to come out and say it. Coach K is probably not the sweet hoops coach/business genius/grandfather-of-five that he, the media, the Duke basketball information office, Nike, Chevy, and American Express would like you to believe he is. In truth, he's probably kind of a jerk. Or a nickname-for-Richard. Take your pick.

Of all the high-profile coaches in the games, is there one you'd less like to spend a night drinking beer and playing Boggle with?

Okay, Rick Barnes, but after that? Really think about it for a minute.

On the likeability index, Coach K rates somewhere between Chris Brown and whoever runs Uzbekistan's intelligence agency.

Krzyzewski is prickly. He takes himself way too seriously. His ego is inflated. He must be a little paranoid—a fingerprint scan is required to open the elevator doors to his office. No one would describe his sense of humor as "winning." He seems constantly in a bad mood and is quick to anger. He once told the media that he agreed with a player's assessment that his teammates were all a bunch of "fucking babies."

In the Old West, he'd be called "ornery." He's like one of

Children are warned to
refrain from reading this
man's lips during games.
(Courtesy of Rob Goodlatte)

those villainous dads from every high-school movie—the retired
military man who makes his son's life miserable because of his
unbending code of discipline. Hell, he probably uses military
time. ("Practice is at oh-nine-hundred, sharp!")

Here's a fun little exercise you can do yourself. Pull up a
Google images search for "Mike Krzyzewski" and look what you
come up with. See all those photos of him frowning or yelling?
Keep scanning. Do you see any of him smiling? We mean, aside
from his official university head shot where they probably ordered him to seem halfway cuddly? Do you see any candid photos of him on the sideline, out in the real world or at a press
conference smiling? You don't. He looks downright constipated
in most of the pictures.

But so what? He's an intense guy, we get it. That's probably,
in part, how he's able to win so many games.

And that would be just fine, except that like so much when it comes to Duke, there's an element of hypocrisy here. You don't have to look too deep into Coach K before you realize that there's a huge disconnect between the guy's public image and the real person. Here's a man who the *Sporting News* dubbed "what's right about sports." Here's a man who's beatified during practically every telecast. Here's a man who smugly intoned during his awful American Express TV commercial a few years ago, "I don't look at myself as a basketball coach. I look at myself as a leader who happens to coach basketball."

And when it comes to leadership, this guy is clearly more Dick Nixon than George H. W. Bush.

"I guess the thing that surprised me the most was you don't realize how much he curses and how much he's on the refs all the time," says former UNC guard Bobby Frasor. "I remember someone telling me about [former Duke player] Taylor King during his freshman year and how he thought his name was 'motherfucker,' because that's how Coach K got his attention. I don't know how true it is. I mean, he's a great coach and I'm not going to deny that at all, but the way he handles his players or acts with the refs and media, sometimes it kind of rubs people the wrong way."

A *New York Post* reporter, sitting behind Duke's bench during a 2005 game, described the proceedings during a team huddle thusly:

"Krzyzewski himself was an unfiltered Chris Rock concert for much of the day, but one of his assistants was worse. During one time-out, with the starters sitting on the bench, gulping Gatorade, this was his idea of 'coaching' them: 'You're a bleep, and you're a bleep, and you're a bleeping bleep-bleeper of a bleeper-bleeper. You bleepers don't bleeping deserve to wear the bleeping colors of Duke University! Bleep! Are you bleeping bleeping me? Bleep all of you. Get out of my bleeping faces.'

"At which point, he was replaced by Krzyzewski, whose assessment was far more succinct: 'You bleeping make me bleeping sick.'"

That's more bleeps than a Source Awards telecast.

"His mouth is terrible. He has that reputation. You don't want kids sitting behind the bench, that's for sure," says former UNC guard Dewey Burke. "It takes a certain kind of player to deal with that over the course of four years. As players sitting around, yeah, we'll talk about how I don't know how I could play for a guy like that."

One of Coach K's tried-and-true motivating tactics is reportedly to completely blast the freshmen and other weak-link players during practice, only to later send a senior over to the player's room to explain why he was so angry.

After a particularly poor 2005 workout, during which Coach K reamed his players in front of more than two hundred invited guests, including NCAA president Myles Brand, forward Lee Melchionni told *Sports Illustrated,* "That's one thing about the Duke program: You're always going to get the absolute truth from Coach. You may go back to your dorm room and cry, but you're going to come back the next day and be better because of it."

And it's not just his players that he can be peevish with. It's also members of the media, whose existence Coach K seems to barely tolerate.

How many other head coaches won't deign to spend fifteen seconds with the designated TV sideline reporter at halftime, dispatching a lowly assistant instead?

"I don't agree with coaches doing that. It's a philosophical thing," Coach K has said. "The only people I should talk to are my players."

About the only time anyone gets access to the coach is during the postgame press conference, which can often turn churlish.

"Obviously, you didn't see the game tonight, okay?" Krzyzewski snapped, interrupting a journalist who was asking about Duke losing a lead during a 2004 game versus UConn. "Which question would you want me to answer?" he later barked.

During a 2008 press session for the U.S. Olympic team, the coach ridiculed a foreign journalist who asked in hesitant English whether the American team was showing off by dunking too much.

"There was no showing off," K said defensively, glaring at the journalist. "You dunk when you have to dunk. Maybe it's a difference in our languages. Maybe in your language playing hard means showing off."

And then there was Krzyzewski's most infamous run-in with the media—the student media, that is. In 1990, the coach blew his stack after a student sports reporter in the university newspaper dared to give his team a B+ midseason grade.

He summoned ten newspaper staffers to the locker room and let loose with an eight-minute profanity-laced tirade that would have given a gentler man a stroke.

Unbeknownst to K, one of the reporters secretly recorded the blowup with a tape recorder hidden in his bag.

Coach K began by calling the midseason report card "full of shit," and went on to whine, "I just wonder where your mind-set is that you don't appreciate the kids in this locker room. I'm not looking for puff pieces or anything like that, but you're whacked out and you don't appreciate what the fuck is going on and it pisses me off—and I'm suggesting that if you want to appreciate what's going on—get your head out of your ass and start looking out for what's actually happening."

Another coach might have been fired for a blue-streaked outburst against—again—*student* reporters. And not only students, but ones at his own school. But Coach K's reputation took only the slightest ding. Dick Vitale was probably on the air that very night gushing about how much K does for charity.

But let's face facts. The dude is just plain mean.

When Nick Collison, who was heavily recruited by Duke, called Krzyzewski to tell him he was going to Kansas, K didn't exactly wish him well. Or even pretend to. "He was like, 'I don't care. We got a commitment from Casey Sanders anyway,'" Collison told Kusports.com. (Sanders, a six-foot-eleven center, averaged 2.7 points for his career. Collison, meanwhile, currently plays for the Oklahoma City Thunder.)

During a 2005 Duke–North Carolina game at Chapel Hill, Coach K became incensed by a fan who yelled, "You've got [referee] Larry Rose in your pocket!" The coach had security move the fan farther away from the bench, according to the *New York Post*. The fan later turned out to be Scott Williams, son of UNC coach Roy Williams. Oops.

Anyone want to hire this guy to entertain children at a birthday party?

Why don't Krzyzewski's accomplishments come with a big, fat, shiny asterisk? Why does the man continue to be canonized in the media, while his surly side gets buried? Does winning basketball games make him that bulletproof?

No one is asking Coach K to become soft and cuddly, or even to clean up his language. His players, at least the ones that don't transfer, seem to like—or at least tolerate—his raw approach, and far be it from us to question that. But why can't a fuller picture of the coach be presented, so that we, the public, can form our own opinions, free of all the manufactured BS that Duke, Coach K, the media, and the advertisers want to shove down our throats?

When Yankees owner George Steinbrenner—another sports figure who was known to be demanding and prickly—died in 2010, his obituaries presented him as he was, warts and all. *The New York Times* recounted his felony conviction and the way he had been "overbearing and even verbally abusive" toward his children.

We can hope for nothing less for Coach K. But why wait until he passes away? No time like the present to start setting the record straight.

Verdict: What's former VP Cheney's first name again?

CHARGE #10

DUKE WOULD NOT PLAY A TRUE ROAD GAME AGAINST A QUALITY OPPONENT IF COACH K'S VERTEBRAE DEPENDED ON IT.

If you're not familiar with the term *helicopter parent,* it doesn't mean moms and dads in those cute little hats with spinners on the top who write software programs by day and watch *Doctor Who* reruns by night. It means parents who are overinvolved in their children's lives. Way overinvolved. These aren't the parents who are holding their kids' hands as they walk into preschool; these are the parents who are holding their kids' hands as they walk into college.

When you start to look at Duke's basketball schedule over the last several years, it's a spot-on analogy to helicopter parents: overly protective. Ridiculously micromanage-y. And scared to death that even the slightest adversity could befall Junior.

Scheduling a season is no simple task. A team is always required to play a certain number of games in its own conference, and those are set years in advance. Outside of that, a program has any number of choices for early-season mini-tournaments in locales like Anchorage, New York City, Maui, Puerto Rico, and other places that give coaches a chance to wear ugly cruisewear on national television. (Note to anyone who ever wants to be taken seriously again: Hawaiian shirts are not a good idea.)

But those games are all on neutral floors. If it's smart, a

program also wants to schedule a reasonable amount of out-of-conference opponents that really test its team's mettle. We won't even give Duke too much grief for scheduling the occasional cream puff outside of conference play. All teams throw a few sacrificial lambs in there. (What's up, Gardner-Webb!) But look closer. Duke hardly ever plays true away games unless they are forced to.

Ever.

By "true away games," we are talking about games played on an opponent's home floor. Not at an arena down the highway. Not at a football stadium in the same state. At your opponent's arena, on its floor, with its rims, its banners hanging in the rafters, its fans filling the seats, and its overpriced hot dogs stinking up the concourse.

Playing true road games gives a team a sense of being behind enemy lines. It's a test for a team's toughness. And Duke avoids them like we avoid watching reality shows about midgets falling in love. For a supposed elite program, Duke really, really plays a suspiciously small amount of road games out of conference.

Oh, they'll claim they do. They'll claim they go on the road just as much as other clubs, but this is not exactly true. The Devils like to pull a little sleight of hand when it comes to an "away" game. They'll play outside the comfy confines of Cameron, but they'll insist the game be moved to some large, neutral arena. Like taking on Oregon but playing at the Rose Garden in Portland.

In the late 1980s and early 1990s, Duke played four regular-season games against the Arizona Wildcats. The Devils lost both that were played in Arizona. So when it came to scheduling a new set of contests a few years ago, what did Coach K and the Duke admin suggest? You guessed it: a neutral-site contest in New Jersey (which to be honest is like playing in Cameron for Duke).

The offer was soundly rejected by 'Zona coach Lute Olson.

"I said, 'You know what? We'll play the neutral-site game in Phoenix or the Pond [of Anaheim, CA],'" Olson told the *Arizona Daily Star* in 2004. "'But other than that, you just call Duke up and tell them to go fly a kite.'"

Duke will surely say that the move is done to make more money. That you can get more spectators in the local NBA hall as opposed to the sweatbox on campus. We call it BS. They're scared, plain and simple. Their schedule is about nothing more than padding their stats to gain that inevitable number one seed in the NCAAs.

Take a look at the ten seasons from 2001 to 2011 alone. Figure that Duke plays roughly twenty-five to thirty regular-season games with sixteen of those being conference games. So that leaves about ten games to schedule out of conference (disregarding contractual obligations, like the Big Ten—ACC Challenge). That means we are talking about approximately one hundred games out of 250 to 300 total. How many of those games do you think are actual *true* away games?

Sit down for this. The following is a stone-cold fact. The *total* number of true away games is . . . wait for it . . . *three*. Total. Not per year. Total. We can't freaking believe this.

It gets even better when you look at the outcomes. On December 6, 2008, they lost 81–73 to Michigan in Ann Arbor. On January 21, 2006 (yes, that is almost a three-year gap), they lost 87–84 to Georgetown in Washington, D.C. And on December 8, 2001 (a four-year gap), they beat Michigan 104–83 in Ann

Arbor. They were a whopping 1-2. Oh, and that one win? That was a year in which Michigan was ranked 151st in the RPI at the time they played Duke and went on to finish 5-11 in the Big Ten and 11-18 overall.

Over that same time span, they played a ridiculous fourteen times in Madison Square Garden in New York City and four times in East Rutherford, New Jersey. Um, that ain't no away game for the University of New Jersey at Durham.

For the sake of comparison, let's also look at North Carolina's schedules over the last ten years and see how many true away games they played. Actually, screw it. We don't need to look at ten years of data; we only need to look at a sixteen-day span in December of 2007 to equal Duke's number. UNC played at Kentucky on December 1, at the University of Pennsylvania on December 4, came home and took exams, and then played at Rutgers on December 16. Their record was three wins and zero losses.

Let's repeat that for those readers from Alabama who may be math-challenged. UNC played as many true away games in two and a half weeks as Duke did in ten years. In fact, UNC averaged nearly two true away games per year, playing a total of eighteen over that same span of seasons.

It's disgusting isn't it?

When we spoke with ESPN bracketologist Joe Lunardi, he said, "This is a legitimate factual reason to hate Duke, if I were to take your side of it. Each year, I give the Rand McNally award for the team that goes the longest in a season without playing a true road game. Duke has won it more than once."

And the most ironic part about it is that a good argument could be made that this road avoidance ends up biting Duke in the ass most years come tournament time. The minute they get into unfriendly environs, they get beat.

So why keep doing it? Why keep avoiding away games like NBA scouts avoided Nick Horvath?

It reeks of a mentality of overprotectiveness. In other words, Duke sets its basketball schedules like a bunch of helicopter parents. And do you know what happens to the kids of helicopter parents when they finish their four to five years of carefully moderated, micromanaged, cocooned schooling? They move right back in with their parents, of course.

Which, come to think of it, perfectly explains the makeup of the current Blue Devil assistant coach ranks. Chris Collins, Wojo, Jeff Capel, Nate James, and the rest of you dark-blue-suited wannabes, you're the basketball equivalent of a thirty-three-year-old loser living in his parents' basement. Time to move the hell out.

Verdict: Guilty with aggravating circumstances. It's time to cut the cord and put together a schedule like your boys have a pair.

EXHIBIT D

TOP 12 MOST HUMILIATING MOMENTS

1938

Anyone who's watched Dookies flop around like French mimes knows the team has a gift for dramatic acting, and the Blue Devils may trace the talent back to Fred Edwards. In a 1938 contest against Florida, Edwards is stripped of the ball by a defender. But instead of running the other way, the Dookie continues toward his own basket while pretending to dribble a ball he no longer has. He then simulates a shot, as the crowd convulses with laughter.

JANUARY 6, 1940

Duke fans will not want you to know this. You won't find the information in the university's official online literature, but when Duke Indoor Stadium—now known as Cameron—was dedicated back in 1940, the keynote address was delivered by none other than the dean from the University of North Carolina, Robert B. House. Yes, an official from Duke's most hated rival was the person who dedicated their beloved Cameron. That's one of those historical sports black marks that will never wash off, kind of like the Red Sox trading the Babe. Things quickly got more embarrassing for the Dookies. A fuse blew, killing the power in the new arena and stranding dozens of VIPs and city officials in the dark.

FEBRUARY 9, 1957

During a heated game between North Carolina and Duke, the Blue Devils storm back to tie the score at 73 with a few seconds left. Because the scoreboard is manually operated and slow to change, the points do not immediately register. Duke player Bobby Joe Harris, thinking his team is still down by two, fouls UNC's Tommy Kearns, who goes to the line and makes both. Carolina wins 75–73. "It still bothers me," Harris would say years later. "What a terrible way to lose a game."

MARCH 11, 1983

The Blue Devils get absolutely blown out of the building by Virginia in the ACC tournament. Despite being down just 9 at halftime, Duke goes on to lose 109–66. The 43-point loss remains the largest margin of defeat ever in the tournament.

MARCH 31, 1990

During a Final Four game against Arkansas, Bobby Hurley runs to the locker room multiple times to attend to some, er, business. The press is happy to leave his ailment at "stomach flu," but Coach K—God knows why—is quick to clarify during the postgame press conference. "Bobby had a lot of problems physically," he says. "He had diarrhea. Is there any other word for that?"

SEPTEMBER 28, 1990

Former Dookie Jay Bilas tries his hand at acting (and we use that term loosely) by appearing in the sci-fi dud *Dark Angel* (aka *I*

Jay Bilas and his sweet mullet helped defeat evil in *I Come in Peace*.
(Courtesy of Metro-Goldwyn-Mayer Studios, Inc.)

Come in Peace), one of those movies destined for the five-dollar discount bin even before its release. Appearing alongside lunkhead Dolph Lundgren, Bilas plays an alien cop decked out in a terrible mullet and what appears to be a Members Only jacket from the year 2079. The film grosses just $1.9 million in its opening weekend and gets savaged by critics. The one saving grace is that Bilas isn't really required to speak through most of the movie.

JANUARY 26, 2005

You live by the cheer sheet, you die by the cheer sheet. In an operation worthy of the CIA or Israel's Mossad, a rival student manages to plant some false information on the Dookies' beloved cheer sheets, pulling off one of the greatest anti-Duke pranks of all time. The rival spy instant-messages Duke's head line monitor Steve Rawson that he had some compromising information about Maryland star Nik Caner-Medley. The Terrapin, the spy says, has a girlfriend named Myra, whose pet name for Caner-Medley was "Piggy." The Maryland star hates the nickname the source insists, so it would really get under his skin to cheer "Myra 'n' Piggy" during the Duke–Maryland game. What the Duke students are too dense to figure out is that the cheer sounds an awful lot like Myron Piggie, the name of the disgraced AAU coach who went to jail for paying high-school players, including Duke's own Corey Maggette. The full chant never materializes during the game, but single chants of "Piggy" are heard and at least one sign reading PIGGY is spotted in the crowd at Cameron. The prank led Duke's head line monitor in 2006 to ban cheer-sheet suggestions that were submitted via e-mail or Instant Messenger.

FEBRUARY 5, 2005

Coach K gets so worked up during a game at Cameron, that he gets dizzy, drops to his knees, then keels over on his side. And what was he doing at the time? Why, chewing out the officials, of course. The embarrassed coach, fortunately, is fine (we'd never wish serious health problems on the guy, though a little diarrhea would be okay) and says he just got a bit woozy. "I've got to deal with that forever now," Krzyzewski said after the game. "I felt like a chump, like somebody hit me with an air punch. I'm thinking, 'What an idiot.' I know I'm going to get it from my wife and my daughters. They have so much ammunition on me now."

FEBRUARY 28, 2005

The FleetCenter has the bright idea to auction off "naming rights for a day" on eBay. The winning bidder will supposedly be allowed to choose a name for the facility, and the new moniker will appear on the Jumbotron during a Boston Celtics game, on the arena's Web site and in a message that greets callers on the automated phone system. Drew Curtis, the man behind news aggregator Fark.com, places the top bid of $2,550 and announces that the FleetCenter will now be called the "Fark.com Duke Sucks Center." Unamused officials reject the idea. Curtis ultimately had to settle on "Boston Garden," the old, precorporate name for the stadium.

MARCH 15, 2007

When the vastly superior Blue Devils are shocked by unknown eleventh seed VCU (Virginia Commonwealth University) in the first round of the NCAA tournament, Coach K downplays the significance of the embarrassing collapse. "The real story is that we've been in the tournament every year since 1996, not that we lost in the first round," he said. "The fact that these kids played well enough to put us in a position to lose a first-round game is the story." No, we're pretty sure losing in the first round was the real story.

MARCH 8, 2008

When UNC forward Danny Green dunks on—and we mean *on*—Duke guard Greg Paulus, it isn't just a posterization. It's a full-on gigantic wall mural, like the kind painted on the side of a stadium. This was possibly one of the most vicious dunks in the history of the Duke–UNC rivalry. With 2:41 left in the first half at Cameron, Green grabs the rebound from an errant Duke shot, dribbles, dishes to Marcus Ginyard, who gives it right back to Green. Paulus, who is the lone man back, positions himself under the basket, and like every good Dookie, prepares to do what he does best: flop. Green pays the gnat no mind. He goes straight up and through the defender, hammering down the ball, and knocking a helpless Paulus backward. "That felt good, man," Green would say. "There are a lot of people around the country that don't like Greg Paulus. I'm pretty sure a lot of those people were rooting for me right there."

AUGUST 1, 2011

Duke officials sheepishly announce (on a summer Saturday when coincidentally no one is paying attention to the news) that they were looking into a possible recruiting violation committed by Coach K. The "leader who just happens to coach basketball" allegedly offered a scholarship to forward Alex Poythress during an AAU tournament—a violation of NCAA regulations. At press time, the investigation was still ongoing, but no one had better hold their breath. We refer you to the Corey Maggette investigation.

CHARGE #11

THE MEDIA ARE A BUNCH OF SLOBBERING, PRO—BLUE DEVILS FOOLS WHO LAY AWAKE NIGHTS FANTASIZING ABOUT RUNNING THEIR FINGERS THROUGH COACH K'S DOWNY TOUPEE.

Sports are all about an equal playing field. Honest competition is applauded, while anyone suspiciously growing steroid-fueled man-boobs as big as Mark McGwire's are run out of town.

But that's only during the actual game. When it comes to the media, coverage can be as slanted as a fun-house floor. For decades, fans have complained about a perceived bias toward Duke in radio, newspaper, and especially TV coverage. Writers and announcers fall all over themselves to praise Duke, trotting out the same tired clichés and platitudes year after year. Just like on the court, in the media, the Blue Devils get all the calls, it seems.

But is this perceived bias just a case of rival fans seeing what they want to see, or is there something to it?

"With Duke, it's subjective, but I do think there's a certain media bias," says Pam Laucella, an assistant professor and the academic director at Indiana University's National Sports Journalism Center. Laucella says that bias often manifests itself more in what fans don't see than what they do.

"Certain teams and coaches aren't covered as critically as others," she says. "[TV commentators] are always saying that Duke wins the right way, but there's that stuff with [Chris] Duhon's mom being given a job and Corey Maggette being paid as a high-school player. Duke basketball is just put on a pedestal."

It's true. Ask yourself, how much coverage do you remember about Duke's various basketball scandals over the years? Not much, probably. Now think about how much coverage you've had to endure about how great the Cameron Crazies are. Point made.

"Coach K probably protects the program to a certain degree and the sports information department to some degree," Laucella says. "It's like kind of a cocoon. They don't let a lot of stuff leak out."

"In journalism in general and sports in particular, there really is no such thing as this ideal of impartiality that we like to believe in," says Brad Schultz, a University of Mississippi associate professor of journalism and the founding editor of the *Journal of Sports Media*. "The people who cover the games are human beings, and they have prejudices and favorites and biases, just like anyone else."

The biggest, most super-scintillating-sensational favorites-player is Dick Vitale, the excitable ESPN color man who seems to go out of his way to mention Duke at least twice a broadcast, even during games in which the Blue Devils aren't playing. In the 99.9 percent of their games he does call, he gushes in a veritable Niagara Falls of alliterative hyperbole about Duke's great players (bonus points for giving them douchey nicknames), the creative Cameron Crazies, the student's SAT scores, Coach K, Coach K's family, Coach K's wife, Coach K Court, Krzyzewskiville, the campus, the arena, the library, whatever he happened to have eaten at the cafeteria earlier that day, and on and on and on, until the audience at home is tempted to change the channel. Or sell their TV altogether.

Vitale's grandchildren have even been spotted in the stands at a Virginia Tech game wearing Blue Devils gear, a photo posted on truthaboutduke.com revealed. The commentator's pro-Duke antics got so out of hand that Coach K reportedly asked him to tone it down, because Vitale was causing even more hatred to be heaped on the program.

Vitale hasn't really ever disputed that he's in the tank for the Devils. His stance has been that there's nothing to criticize. (Guess the dude hasn't seen Duke's cheerleaders.)

Vitale addressed the bias issue at a 2009 charity gala, telling the crowd, "I have been accused of singing the praises of Duke and singing the praises of North Carolina and I will never apologize for that. Number one, I think I am being honest for that and very candid in my evaluation. If I am singing the praises of a program that has fourteen wins a year, then you have a right to complain. But when I am talking about a team and program that year after year is winning games, graduating players, in the challenge for a national championship, I have no problem with that whatsoever . . . But I will tell you this, there is no doubt that we try to be honest and try to be fair."

And this from a man who prior to a 2009 Duke–Villanova tournament game gushed, "This game was won three years ago when Gerald Henderson picked Duke over Villanova." Dookie V, as the announcer is known, then went on to assure the audience that the Blue Devils had this one in the bag.

Duke ended up getting killed 77–54, with Henderson going one-for-fourteen and scoring seven points. Good call, Dickie.

Schultz says that a lot of biased sports coverage could result from a conscious or unconscious attempt to curry favor with a team or its players. (Coach K is notoriously media-averse and rarely gives interviews beyond an irritable postgame press conference.)

"In the case of the Vitale," Schultz says, "he may have a personal relationship with Duke, or he may want to create a personal relationship with Duke in order to get access. That's a lot of it, too. Access determines a lot of this. You have to have access, and a lot of what's said and written revolves around creating and maintaining access to players and teams."

Duke also may benefit from the bandwagon effect, the idea that people do or believe certain things just because everyone else does. In other words, the more the media talk about how great Duke is, the more people believe it. And the more people believe it, the more they talk about it, and the more the media write about it.

"In the technological world, you'd talk about something going viral—something that catches people's imaginations or attention, so everybody else has got to talk about it," Schultz says. "If everybody else is talking about it and you [as a media outlet] are not talking about it, you're not serving your audience, and that's the ultimate goal for any sports journalist."

Take, for example, the coverage J. J. Redick got when he wore Duke blue. Vitale dubbed him nothing short of the greatest shooter in the country. Duke's then-assistant coach Mike Jarvis II said he was "Derek Jeter with a jump shot." Coach K claimed J. J. was the best shooter he ever coached. "Perfect Jumper Faithful Sidekick to Duke's Redick" trumpeted a typical headline in the North Carolina paper *News & Record*.

Sorry to intrude with reality, but during his senior year in

2005–06, which was his best as a Blue Devil, Redick ranked a forgettable twenty-second in the NCAA in three-point percentage. In free-throw percentage, he was twenty-fifth. Redick wasn't the best shooter in the nation. He just happened to be the best shooter that played for Duke.

In 2005, Arizona's coach Lute Olson decided to call out the media on its pro-Duke slant. Fed up with the eternal Redick love parade, Olson made the wacky suggestion that Arizona's Salim Stoudamire deserved the title of best shooter in the country based on, you know, stats and junk.

"There's a bit of information that [was] shared with me about Redick being the greatest shooter in the country," Olson said. "If he hit seventy-one consecutive field goals, he'd reach Salim's field-goal percentage shooting. If Redick made fifty-three consecutive three-pointers, he'd tie Salim for three-point field-goal percentage. How in the world can somebody continue to go on TV and say Redick is the greatest shooter in the country?"

Blame the bandwagon effect, Lute.

Illinois' Bruce Weber also took issue with all the pro-Duke histrionics. During an August 2005 pep rally, the coach was touting his team's sterling 75-3 home record over the previous three seasons. "That's not just the best record in the Big Ten; it's the best in the nation. So Dick Vitale can take his Dookies and shove it."

All this pro-Duke bias may seem harmless enough. So what? The worst that can happen is the university gets a little more ink or fed-up viewers spend hours finding a way to sync their radios to their TVs so they won't have to listen to Dookie V anymore. But like all media bias, prejudice in sports media has consequences. They may not be as dire as those arising from, say, journalists not checking into that whole-war-in-Iraq thing, but there are consequences nonetheless.

In Duke's case, the media bias basically creates a loop that goes around and around, possibly forever—or at least until Coach K passes away and is stuffed and placed in the entrance to Cameron in order to scare children of opposing teams.

"Duke has money, Duke has prestige, Duke gets favorable media coverage, so now, because of these resources, they can go out and get the best players and they keep winning," Schultz says. "When you're winning, all these other factors conspire to keep you winning. Once you get to that elite level, it's really kind of cyclical. Money, resources, media attention, victories. And then it kind of starts over again."

Duke wins (or has won), and so they're constantly on television. Because they're constantly on television and announcers are constantly droning on about them, journalists cover them. And because journalists cover them, the team's profile is much higher than most other Division I universities, meaning the school is more likely to land top recruits. Meaning, they're more likely to win. And so on. It's like a snake eating its tail. Or Chris Collins actually trying to cram his head up his ass.

The difficult truth is that Duke will probably never be a second-tier program. The media are going to make sure of it.

Verdict: The sports media is less-than-awesome, baby.

CHARGE #12

COACH K USES SIX POUNDS OF LAMPBLACK ON HIS HAIR PER WEEK.

Not to get too conspiratorial on anyone, but what are the chances that Coach K is actually dead?

Hear us out on this one.

We're not exactly sure when it happened. We're not exactly sure how it happened. Maybe he died in a car accident twenty years ago. Maybe he keeled over last week from a brain hemorrhage brought on by a particularly violent cussing of Wojo for using too little starch.

However it happened, it happened. He expired. He went to that Great Back-Treatment Facility in the Sky.

And after he died, Duke University, afraid of losing big-time recruits and even bigger-time donors, hatched a diabolical plan. They would replace him with an amazingly lifelike animatronic figure, like the ones performing nightly at a Chuck E. Cheese near you. (Only one that looked more rodentlike.)

And it is that robot that has been roaming Duke's sidelines for years.

It's far-fetched—maybe—but how else to possibly explain this man's hair? It is ridiculously, unnaturally black. It is not only black; it's Huey P. Newton black. Jet-black. Ink-black. It is the complete absence of light. If it were a crayon color, it would be called What the Universe Looked Like Before the Big Bang. Even Germans won't wear shirts this black.

For years, fans and haters have speculated about Krzyzewski's hair, mainly because he is (at the time of this writing) sixty-four years old and still has a head of hair that looks like the floor of a Japanese barbershop. True, it's a little thinner than it used to be, and it has receded a bit on the sides, but the color has remained unchanged since he began coaching at Duke back in the Mesozoic Era.

Name us another sixty-four-year-old man who has hair this black. Name us another forty-four-year-old man who does.

What mysteries lie in the inky blackness of Coach K's hair?
(Courtesy of West Point Public Affairs)

The conclusion is obvious: He's dyeing his hair. He has single-handedly kept Just For Men in business for the past two decades, stockpiling cases of its "Real Black" flavor like Armageddon nuts stockpile canned goods and firearms.

K denies that there's any enhancement going on up top. "I'm going bald so, uh, I am going a little gray [at the temples]," he said at a 2007 press conference. "People think I color my hair. I don't color my hair. Well, my mom had dark hair. She had it for a long, long time."

This hair-coloring rumor has been dogging Krzyzewski for

years, so in the effort of fairness, we decided to try and get to the bottom of it.

First, we called a few drugstores in the Durham area to see if anyone working there had ever spotted Coach K sneaking in three minutes before closing time to pick up a bottle of antacid, a tube of hemorrhoid cream, and a five-gallon drum of hair dye.

Unfortunately, those stores hung up on us.

Next, we went to David Velasco, a Pennsylvania salon owner and the author of *Trade Secrets of a Haircolor Expert*. Velasco studied hundreds of photos of Coach K and rendered his opinion.

Better hold on to something tight for this one.

Velasco says that K most likely does not dye his hair. You read that right. That mop of inky night on the top of his head could actually be natural.

It was the gray hairs that tipped off Velasco. Upon close examination, Coach K has a handful scattered across his head, and Velasco says it's impossible to get a dye job that leaves a few random gray hairs like this. His hair also doesn't show any discoloring in the roots, especially through his part, where you'd expect to see gray creeping in.

And finally, Velasco says that color-treated hair often develops a reddish cast some two to three weeks after treatment because of something called "the oxidation process." We don't know what that is or want to; we're not in beauty school. But the bottom line is, Krzyzewski's hair has never shown any of this reddish tint.

"I know what you and everyone else are probably thinking," Velasco says, "that there is no way that a sixty-four-year-old man could have hair this dark, but it is quite common especially given his ethnic origin. Many Polish people have dark hair and darker skin."

We realize you're disappointed. We know we were. But it's fine, really. The point is, K and his team of given us enough real reasons to despise them over the years, that none of us need ever stoop to making ones up.

Oh, but there is one more thing, if you're feeling especially petty. While K may not dye his hair, Velasco says the coach's head does show evidence of a very good transplant job, which is betrayed by the curious way his hairline is receding. But that's just his guess.

Feel better now?

Verdict: We can't believe we're saying this, but innocent. That hair, like his creative use of the F-word, is all Coach K.

CHARGE #13

"THE STOMP" MANAGED TO ENCAPSULATE EVERYTHING WE HATE ABOUT DUKE IN A SINGLE, AWFUL MOMENT: DICKISH BEHAVIOR, AN ENTITLED MENTALITY, PREFERENTIAL TREATMENT, SELECTIVE MEMORY LOSS BY THE MEDIA, AND FLOPPY HAIR.

Attention, Kentucky fans. If you have been asked by your doctor to avoid activities that will significantly raise your blood pressure, you might want to skip this chapter. (You should also lay off the pork rinds.) Sure, we are about to cover an incident that happened twenty years ago but most Kentucky fans we know still haven't gotten over it. To them, it is known as "The Stomp." And it probably wouldn't be evoking a post-traumatic stresslike reaction from Wildcat followers if the "stomp*er*" hadn't later gone on to hit "The Shot" in what many call The Greatest College Basketball Game Ever Played.

For the uneducated, here's what went down before Christian Laettner's foot, well, went down. With less than nine minutes to go in the second half of the Eastern Regional Final between Duke and Kentucky, the Blue Devils push their lead to nine. A berth in the Final Four is on the line. Laettner gets the ball on the right block and turns to drive for the layin. A skinny, little-used Kentucky freshman named Aminu Timberlake slides over to try to take a charge but gets there late. Laettner misses the shot, and a blocking foul is called. Dead ball.

Laettner turns to walk toward the free-throw line and sees Aminu Timberlake sprawled out on the floor under the basket, and intentionally takes his right foot and stomps down on Timberlake's chest.

This is not up for debate.

Laettner admitted that he did it on purpose in the ESPN Classic *Battle Lines* show about the game, saying, "I thought he had pushed me on the other end of the court. It was just a stupid reaction-type thing. And sure, I wanted to stomp a lot harder but I knew that would be really, really dumb. I wanted to let him know that I wasn't going to take any crap. And there's nothing wrong with adding a little spice to the game."

That little dash of pretty-boy paprika only garnered a technical foul in the game, and this is where Kentucky fans go off the deep end. Clearly, it was an intentional act that had no place in the game. It was not during the course of action but after a whistle and Laettner easily could have been (and probably should have been) ejected. The game later went into overtime where Laettner scores Duke's final eight points including The Shot after a three-quarter-court pass from Grant Hill at the buzzer. He finished the game with thirty-one points on ten-for-ten shooting.

Afterward, Duke teammate Cherokee Parks told Bill Lyon at *The Philadelphia Inquirer* that he wasn't at all surprised to see the cheap shot. "It's so Laettner. He's supposed to be like this All-America, this glamour boy, Mr. GQ. If you know Laettner, it's such a Laettner move to do something like that."

In an interview with *Sports Illustrated*'s Grant Wahl in 2001, Aminu Timberlake downplayed the incident. "Maybe he should've gotten tossed," Timberlake said, laughing. "But I can't change history. To me, it always looked worse than it really was."

Fine, Aminu. Maybe you can't change history. But let's give it a shot anyway. Here are a few more facts to chew on.

Laettner finished the game with four personal fouls in an era in which technical fouls did not count toward a player's personal foul tally. If the incident happened today, he would have fouled out.

Going by the book, Laettner clearly should have been sent to the showers. In Section 23, Article 2 of the NCAA Basketball rulebook for 2010–2011, the rules state that a flagrant technical foul shall result in an automatic ejection. Section 26, Article 1 says that a fight is a flagrant foul while Article 2 defines fighting as "a confrontation involving one or more players, coaches, or other team personnel wherein (but not limited to) a fist, hand, arm, foot, knee, or leg is used to combatively strike the other individual."

Note the word "foot" there, Christian.

If stomping on another player's chest isn't "combative," we don't know what is. By today's definitions, The Stomp would have fallen under the fighting rule and Laettner would have been tossed.

Even if you myopically argue that it wasn't a "fighting" motion, it was most definitely a technical foul after the whistle was blown as a result of a deliberate event. Section 29, Article 3 (which defines technical fouls), subsection F, subsection 1 says that "A flagrant contact technical foul occurs when the ball is dead and the contact is severe (serious, deliberate) or extreme (applied to the greatest degree)."

In 2009, a very similar incident occurred during a regular season game between Houston and Arizona. With 9:51 left in the game and Houston up 63–51, Houston's Aubrey Coleman was called for a charge while driving on Arizona's Chase Budinger around midcourt. With Budinger on the floor, Coleman got up and as he stepped over Budinger, stepped on his face and shoulder. If you look at the video, it's debatable whether or not Coleman did it intentionally. He certainly didn't look down before placing his foot like Laettner did.

Nevertheless, he did step on another dude's face. And guess what happened in this game? Coleman was called for a flagrant technical foul and *ejected*. Arizona then came storming back to win the game in overtime, 96–90. We know it wasn't for a chance to go to the Final Four but the similarities are pretty eerie, aren't they?

But in this case, the stomper got tossed and the stompee's team won the game. And what happened afterward? Did Coleman tell ESPN about how he wanted to add some "spice" to the game? Nope. He issued an apology.

"I never meant to step on him," Coleman said. "I have never been in an incident like this before, and I have nothing but respect for him as a great player. I love the game too much to do something like that intentionally. I want to say I am sorry from the bottom of my heart. I know that God knows what is in my heart, but I am hopeful that Chase will understand and forgive."

For us, The Stomp just sums up everything about why Duke sucks and is, in fact, a historical turning point in Duke hatred, as well as the history of college basketball. If Laettner had been tossed out of the game like he should have been, Duke probably loses. He was on fire that day and clearly Duke's best player and their senior leader. Even if Duke managed to scrape through the game, get to overtime, and manage to be down by only one with 1.6 seconds remaining, who takes that final shot? Bobby Hurley? Please.

The next week, Duke went on to beat Indiana and then Michigan in the Final Four to capture their second championship in a row. They were the first repeat champs since John Wooden's UCLA teams of the early 1970s. That victory over Michigan's Fab Five cemented Duke's status as an elite team of the '90s.

We don't want to go all *Back to the Future* on you here but if Laettner isn't there to hit that shot, it doesn't get shown over and over and over and over again every March. (The FCC should require that if CBS wants to show The Shot, they have to also show The Stomp.) Duke doesn't become the symbol of buzzer-beating March Madness. Duke doesn't go on to build a reputation as one of the sport's elite teams and instead begins to fade from view. With no publicity, without the media constantly reinforcing their image, the team would have trouble recruiting elite players, and without top personnel, they eventually would have trouble winning, and the program would become just another decent-enough, midlevel contender with memories of winning a title in its rearview mirror. And maybe Coach K slinks away to coach the some small-market NBA team.

It's easy to imagine an alternate universe in which Laettner was rightfully ejected from the game, setting off a chain reaction that would have derailed the Duke program for years to come . . . maybe forever. On the downside, Michael J. Fox might never have been born.

For many, the Laettner Stomp was the first time the Duke veneer started to wear off on the national stage. Bill Lyon wrote in the *Philadelphia Inquirer* a few days after the game about how this played out to the national sports audience saying, "It was a pouty, adolescent act, gratuitous, designed not to injure but to intimidate and to instigate. He turned his back and walked

away, and it reminded you of the snotty little playground provo-
cateur in grade school who would push from behind and then
run inside."

Perfect. To us, it is just pure, unadulterated Dookieness.

Verdict: Guilty of getting away with some bull that changed
college basketball forever . . . for the worse.

EXHIBIT E

MATCH-THE-QUOTE GAME

Duke players and coaches have said some idiotic, ridiculous, and otherwise head-scratching stuff over the years. Can you figure out who said what?

Foul Miami.
(Courtesy of Rob Goodlatte)

1. "As long as you don't bring your gayness on me I'm fine. As far as business-wise, I'm sure I could play with him. But I think it would create a little awkwardness in the locker room."—A former Duke player on John Amaechi, the NBA's first openly gay player

2. "My life story is read in poetic stages/ I was once weak-minded, now I'm courageous/The cause and effect of a thousand actions/The mathematical breakdown of micro-fractions."—A Dookie's horrific attempt at poetry

3. "No one thinks more highly of me than probably myself. I think that's fine."

4. "The greatest thing is knowing that I loved you and you loved me back."—A Dookie on Coach K

5. "The first couple of weeks here, I didn't eat three meals a day. I sometimes just forgot. Small things like getting a haircut, keeping up your hygiene—things you don't pay attention to because Mom and Dad take care of them."

6. "I sleep with a ball. I carry it wherever I go the day before and day of our games. Whenever I get off a bus, I always have a ball in my hands. I just like to get the feel of it and have great dreams that night. I'm not ever going to say that when I wake up the ball isn't on the floor, but I want it there to have good thoughts when I go to bed."

7. "Coach smiled at me. I was aglow. I thought, 'He likes me. He can tell I'm a good person.' Then he said I had angelic eyes."

A. Christian Laettner
B. Shavlik Randolph
C. Kyle Singler

D. Chris Duhon

E. J. J. Redick

F. DeMarcus Nelson

G. Steve Wojciechowski

Answers: 1: B 2: E 3: A 4: G 5: C 6: D 7: F

CHARGE #14

DUKE'S COACHING TREE IS NOT EXACTLY A MIGHTY OAK.

Every program has a coaching tree, and if you don't know what a coaching tree is, it's sorta like a family tree, but without that great-great-grandfather who fathered a child with a slave.

Coach K was a sapling that grew from the coaching tree of Bobby Knight. Yes, Knight was a successful coach, but would you really want to sit under him on a sunny day? Cheery this man was not. After all, he was a guy who was run out of Indiana for throwing a chair during a game, snapping at students, and (allegedly) choking one of his own players.

So Coach K's roots are already a bit rotten.

But before you get too far in looking at the bark, branches, and leaves of K—those assistants and players he's mentored, then sent on their way into the coaching ranks—you have to first figure out what a successful tree looks like. And you needn't look much further than the other programs in the ACC.

You can always start with Dean Smith.

During the 2008 NBA season, nearly a quarter of the head coaches in the league could trace their lineage back to Smith, according to Basketball Prospectus. Hall of Famer Larry Brown, who played for Smith in the '60s, is the only basketball coach to have won both an NCAA title and an NBA title. Brown counts such protégés as Gregg Popovich and Maurice Cheeks.

Members of the Duke Alumni Coaching Hall of Fame. *(Courtesy of Noah Pollock)*

George Karl is another longtime NBA head coach who learned from Smith. Nate McMillan served under Karl. Mike Brown and P. J. Carlesimo coached under Popovich. Former Smith assistants Roy Williams, Eddie Fogler, and Bill Guthridge all went on to win National Coach of the Year honors as head coaches.

That's not a coaching tree. That's a coaching redwood.

Maryland's Gary Williams counts Randy Ayers, Ed Tapscott, Rick Barnes, Fran Dunphy, and Fran Fraschilla as branches on his tree.

Over in the Big East, Syracuse's Jim Boeheim has influenced Rick Pitino, who then was assisted by Tubby Smith, Billy Donovan, and Herb Sendek. Two of those guys then went on to win national championships as head coaches. (Sorry, NC State fans. It sure as hell wasn't Sendek.)

So, what has the "Leader of Men" at fair Duke University begotten? We humbly place the following into pots of dirt to see how they grow:

Mike Brey—Not shabby. His tree is looking like the one from *A Charlie Brown Christmas*—a bit stunted and ratty around the edges but serviceable in a pinch. And Brey is the best of the Duke saplings. He served as a Duke assistant in the late '80s and early '90s and went on to have a decent run at Notre Dame. But he also worked under legendary Maryland high-school coach Morgan Wootten before he assisted K, so who's to say the modest success Brey has had can be attributed to the Dark Lord? And Mike Brey did not play for Coach K. He spent his college playing days at Northwestern State in Natchitoches, Louisiana, before transferring for his senior year to George Washington. We remain unconvinced.

Quin Snyder—He and his gelled hair sat on the Duke bench in the '90s, before taking a head coaching job at Missouri . . . where he was later forced out midseason after the program made back-to-back NIT appearances and was put on a three-year probation after a string of recruiting violations, including allegedly paying players. He was last seen as an assistant coach in the NBA for Doug Collins, whose son is a current assistant in Durham.

Tim O'Toole—Also served as a Duke assistant in the '90s. His contract was not renewed at Fairfield in 2006 after going 9-19. His program avoided major NCAA violations in a 2004 investigation after several former players accused the coaching staff of giving cash to players, falsifying drug tests, and doing schoolwork for team members. O'Toole went 112-120 in eight seasons.

Bob Bender—The Duke grad served under Coach K from 1983 to 1989. Once he was released into the wild, he led the

University of Washington to a big-time 116-142 record before being shown the door.

Chuck Swenson—Another Duke assistant from the 1980s. Swenson was fired in 1994 after running William & Mary into the ground, going 62-134 over seven seasons.

Tommy Amaker—Is it just us or do alleged violations seem to follow Blue Devils assistants like Duke students stalking the one pretty girl on campus? The former Duke star and longtime assistant went on to head up the Harvard program and was accused of a myriad of recruiting infractions cited in a 2008 *New York Times* article, although he was later cleared after an investigation. That's right. Duke assistants can even get Harvard in trouble.

Mike Dement—The former Duke assistant resigned mid-season at Southern Methodist University in 2004 after going 10-15. He did manage to scratch together an overall record of 138-120 over nine years. Since 2005, he's been the head coach at UNC-Greensboro, where he's amassed just 67 wins to 117 losses.

Roshown McLeod—The former Duke forward was abruptly fired from his assistant coaching job at Indiana in 2010 just one week before the season was to end. Seth Davis tweeted, "IU coach Tom Crean just fired asst Roshown McLeod effective immediately. Must have been pretty bad if he couldn't wait one more week." McLeod was hired as coach of St. Benedict's Prep, but lasted just a single season. He resigned in April 2011 after leading the team to a 13-12 record, despite having two Division I signees on his roster.

David Henderson—The former Duke cocaptain and assistant put together a lovely six-year run at Delaware, winning 85 games and losing 93 before being given the boot in 2006.

Jeff Capel—The onetime Duke guard and assistant was axed by Oklahoma in March 2011 after leading the team to a 27-36 record over the previous two seasons. And yes, his program, too, was investigated by the NCAA for violations involving a player being paid three thousand dollars by a financial adviser linked to Capel's assistant. In spring 2011, he came crawling back to Durham with his tail between his legs.

We could go on, but the stench is starting to get to us.

So, what's left of this tree after firings, probations, NCAA investigations, allegations of falsifying drug tests, and lots and lots of losing? There are no more branches. All the leaves have fallen.

Verdict: Guilty. The K coaching tree is nothing more than a rotting, smelly stump in the middle of a lonely field.

CHARGE #15

DUKE IS PARANOID, AND IT CAN FEEL YOUR HATE BREATHING ON THE BACK OF ITS NECK, ALL WET AND HOT AND SMELLING OF RIBS SAUCE.

Guess who owns the domain name dukesucks.com. Take one guess.

It's Duke University.

Does anyone else find this as mind-boggling as we do? Name one other prestigious university in all of America that has had to snap up domain names lest some hater with passable computer skills park themselves there and start letting the vitriol fly.

Name one other university that even cares enough to bother.

And that's the thing: someone at Duke spent man-hours dealing with this problem. There's no way around that. Funds had to be appropriated. Approvals had to be given. There were probably meetings. Meetings!

But how high up did this decision go? Was the president bothered with it? The dean?

My God. Can you even begin to imagine that moment when some flunky brought the news to whatever wealthy, old white man happened to be in charge?

FADE IN.

INT. STUFFY OFFICE.
Leather is everywhere. It's like all the crappy shoes at Aldo got turned into furniture. An elderly, rotund man reclines at his desk. A nervous flunky enters.

> **FLUNKY**
> Sir?

> **OLD WHITE MAN**
> (to be played by Victor Garber if a movie of this ever gets made)
> Ah, yes. Come in. You must be the fellow I'm to hunt for sport.

> **FLUNKY**
> Um, no, sir. Sir, I have some disturbing news.

> **OLD WHITE MAN**
> Jesus H. Christ. What now? Coach K needs a new practice facility?

> **FLUNKY**
> Er, no.

> **OLD WHITE MAN**
> A new arena?

> **FLUNKY**
> No.

> **OLD WHITE MAN**
> New limo?

> **FLUNKY**
> No.

> **OLD WHITE MAN**
> Bigger logo of his name painted on the
> court?

> **FLUNKY**
> Not that I know of.

> **OLD WHITE MAN**
> Assistant coach stepped in it again?

> **FLUNKY**
> Um, no.

> **OLD WHITE MAN**
> Cheating by the basketball players?

> **FLUNKY**
> No, it's—

> **OLD WHITE MAN**
> Is it the lacrosse team again?

FLUNKY
No.

OLD WHITE MAN [PAUSES]
You may continue.

FLUNKY
Well, sir. There's this thing called the
Internet, and—

OLD WHITE MAN
I know what the Internet is. That's how
I find out about Civil War reenactments.

FLUNKY
Right. It's just that we might want to
consider the possibility that some mis-
creant is going to buy the domain name
dukesucks.com and spread scurrilous information about the university and the
basketball team.

OLD WHITE MAN
What? Why would they do such a thing?

FLUNKY [WIPING THE SWEAT FROM HIS BROW]
Well, sir. There are some people out
there—a minority, for sure, but they're
out there—who just don't like us.

OLD WHITE MAN

Nonsense. No one has ever mentioned such a thing down at the boat club.

FLUNKY

Yes, well. To handle the problem, it would only cost a few dollars. I really think we should get in front of the problem. It could avoid us potential embarrassment down the line.

OLD WHITE MAN

Fine. Call a meeting.

SFX

PHONE RINGING

OLD WHITE MAN

Hang on a sec. Coach K is on the line. Something about a new practice facility.

And . . . scene.

We can't say that's exactly how it happened, but it happened. Somewhere along the line, Duke faced the reality that someone was going to buy dukesucks.com, so they staged a George W. Bush–style preemptive strike and they bought it themselves. Are they really that paranoid, that fragile, that they couldn't possibly take being made fun of on the Internet (where no one makes fun of anything, by the way)?

It just outs them even more as thin-skinned, desperate and zero fun. They're like Anna Nicole Smith's dead husband or Mitt Romney. No one would talk to them if they didn't have money.

Verdict: www.guilty.com

CHARGE #16

DUKE STUDENTS ARE A BUNCH OF WEALTHY, ELITIST PUNKS WHO YOU PROBABLY WOULDN'T WANT TO GET STUCK TALKING TO AT THE POLO MATCH.

To the list of insufferable things about Duke, you can add the nickname that they choose to call themselves: "the Ivy League of the South." Someone get us a bucket, stat.

Yes, the campus was built to be a shameless carbon-copy of Princeton and, yes, students live in "houses," not dorms, just like at Harvard, but c'mon. This whole "Ivy League of" thing is just irritating and meaningless. If someone tells you that Cracker Barrel is the Mesa Grill of the interstate system, you don't actually think Bobby Flay is whipping up the apple butter in the back, do you?

No one would deny that Duke provides a good education. And for fifty-one large per year, it damn well better. But it's pretty simple. If you can get into an Ivy League school, then you should just go to an Ivy League school. If you can't get into an Ivy League school but instead get into Duke, *you still aren't going to a GD Ivy League school.*

So why does Duke continue to perpetrate this myth? Why does the university continue to give off this elitist stink that can be whiffed all the way up the Eastern seaboard? Why not just stand on the fact that Duke is a good school and leave it at that? There should be no need to qualify a school with stupid nick-

names. What's next, bumper stickers that read, DUKE. THE HAR-
VARD OF HIGHWAY 15-501?

"I hated Duke," Shane Battier told *The Washington Times* in
1997. "The Michigan–Duke rivalry is pretty huge, and Duke is
always portrayed as these snot-nosed brats, the school down south.
I bought into that. I did not like Duke at all."

Their pissy attitude seems to stem from a sense of entitlement.
And you know what, why shouldn't it? Just look at the makeup
of Duke's student body. Approximately 51 percent are white, 22
percent Asian, and 10 percent African-American, making up the
three largest ethnic groups. Kumbaya.

But when it comes to socioeconomic diversity, that pie chart
isn't so pretty. Duke students basically come in three categories:
rich, filthy rich, and f-ing Bruce Wayne rich.

"Although minorities are more likely to come from families
of lesser means than whites at Duke, they still come from affluent
backgrounds," wrote the *Duke Chronicle* in 2010. Of the freshmen reporting family incomes in 2001 and 2002, white students
reported the highest average family income of about $230,000 per
year, according to the 2006 Campus Life and Learning Project.
Latinos, Asians, and blacks reported average family incomes of
$170,980, $153,401 and $118,316, respectively. The mean income
for U.S. households in 2001 was $58,208, according to the U.S.
Census Bureau.

But what the hell. When you have the means, spending a
quarter of a million dollars over four years to send your young-
ling to Duke is no big deal. And maybe parents pulling in that
kind of scratch think it sounds good to their golfing and tennis
buddies when they tell them dear little Timmy and Tina Trust-
fund go to Duke. Puh-lease.

According to a 2011 report by *The Chronicle of Higher Education*, Duke is fifth in the ranking of richest schools with fewest poor students. *(Courtesy of Believe Collective)*

So if you thought Duke students are a bunch of spoiled, rich white kids, you're only half right. They're a bunch of spoiled, rich kids—race be damned.

"Is Duke a rich kids' school? Yes, to a certain extent all elite universities are rich kids' schools," student Sam Swartz told *Duke Magazine* in 2008. "So many kids come here from these really rich suburbs. They go to wealthy public or private high schools, and they live these really cloistered lives of privilege in these elite enclaves. They come to Duke, and they see Durham as this impoverished place that they don't want to have anything to do with; they never come into contact with people who force them to think differently."

But there must be an upside. Maybe the student body isn't as economically diverse as one might like, but at least these fine kids from fine homes and fine upbringings are showing off their general fine-ness once they step inside that Gothic hellhole, right?

Not so much.

In case you're just tuning in, 2010 marked a zenith of bad behavior for this Ivy League of the South. There was the underage sibling of a student who was found passed out in a Porta Potty, forcing cancellation of a popular party called Tailgate. That transgression came on the heels of Duke student Karen Owen's so-called "F*&% List" going viral faster than that Chocolate Rain guy. The surprisingly professional PowerPoint-esque presentation about her "horizontal academics" ran down all the guys she'd slept with on campus, as well as their—er—distinguishing personal characteristics. If we recall, the phrase "could not walk the next day" was bandied about. And on Halloween, a fraternity posted sexist party flyers across campus inviting any and all "total sluts" to drop by the house. A similarly juvenile e-mail invite made some lame jokes about Helen Keller.

In November 2010, university president Richard Brodhead was forced to act. (Whoa, whoa, whoa—Dick Brodhead is their president? How many times did he get the crap kicked out of him for lunch money with a name like that? Wow.) Mr. President took the unusual step of sending out a campus-wide e-mail, basically ordering the students to shape up.

"This fall we've had a series of incidents that, at least to a distant public, made the most boorish student conduct seem typical of Duke," he wrote. "Tailgate, a community celebration that regularly veered into excess and even danger, had to be canceled last week. Cartoonish images of gender relations have created offense and highlighted persistent discomforts. Like every other college in America, we have too much drinking on this campus. We've had our eyes opened to the serious costs of apparently harmless fun."

The best part of Dick's e-mail (can we call you Dick? Thanks.) was that he deemed it wise to open with a recollection that a similar note was sent out twenty-five years earlier by then-president Terry Sanford dressing down the students for excessively cursing on television during basketball games. (Guess that missive didn't make it to Coach K's desk, huh?)

So, let's see. Rich? Check. Racially diverse? Sure, but still rich. Entitled? Check. Act like total ass-hats? Check.

"They give off sort of an elitist feel with the way they are. It's not just the basketball program," says former UNC guard Dewey Burke. "Many Duke alums I've met are smug and act as if they're better than you. It really doesn't seem necessary. I've known people from Harvard, from Yale and Penn and Princeton who don't act like that. I can't understand it. To me, it's not just the basketball program. It's the whole school.

"My dad and I were playing in a fun one-day golf tournament, and we got paired up with some guys, and I was wearing golf shoes with a North Carolina logo on them. On the first tee, the guy we were playing with turns to me and says, 'You're not really wearing *those,* are you? I went to Duke. Why would you wear *those*?' I said, 'Well, I'm an alum, and actually I played basketball there.' He goes, 'Really? I didn't realize that.' He was backtracking, but I'd never even met this guy. To me, he should have said,

'Hey, did you go to North Carolina?' It's just a way they approach things."

But this air of elitism also extends to the basketball court. As former UCLA guard Rico Hines told the *Charlotte Observer* in 2001, "People in other programs think they're a little stuck up. I know I hated Duke for a long time. Growing up [in Greenville, North Carolina] watching them on TV, you saw the arrogance in people like Bobby Hurley."

Oh, thanks, Rico. Forgot that one. Arrogant? Double check.

Verdict: Guilty, but with a reduced sentence. The student body is full of rich a-holes who could play the villain in every 1980s movie ever made, but at least they're getting a decent education and the campus shows racial diversity.

EXHIBIT F

DUKE'S ALL-OVERPAID NBA TEAM

5. ELTON BRAND

The forward never quite lived up to the hype, but that never stopped GMs from signing humongo checks in his name. In 2010,

Elton Brand, pictured here stealing millions from the 76ers.
(Courtesy of Keith Allison)

Forbes calculated that, based on Brand's meager contribution, the 76ers should have been paying him $576,000 for the season. What they actually paid him: $14.9 million.

4. BOBBY HURLEY

The former Duke playmaker and NBA bust made more money for doing nothing than about anyone this side of Jerome James. In 1996–97, the scantly used Sacramento guard took home $3.066 million for the season (more than Allen Iverson), meaning he collected about $4,850.50 for every minute played.

3. JAY WILLIAMS

The Bulls guard effectively ended his basketball career in June 2003 after he crashed a motorcycle he was driving without a license and without a helmet. Despite being in violation of his contract, Chicago decided to pay Williams the $7.7 million he was owed for the next two seasons. He never played another minute for them.

2. TRAJAN LANGDON

Cleveland wasted the eleventh pick on the so-called Alaskan Assassin, who then went on to make 38 percent, 43 percent, and 40 percent of his field goals in his three seasons, averaging 5.4 points for his brief career. He still earned about $4.5 million before fleeing overseas. The only thing he assassinated was Cleveland fans' will to live.

1. DANNY FERRY

Ferry was essentially Duke's first modern superstar. He earned first-team All-America honors and was named the player of the year in 1989. As the second pick in the draft (ahead of Shawn Kemp and Vlade Divac), Ferry was paid a ton by the Cavs, raking in $2.6 million his first season. He ultimately pulled down as much as $4.6 million as a veteran, although he never came close to living up to his college pedigree. He averaged 7.0 points and 2.8 rebounds for his career and is considered among the NBA's bigger disappointments.

CHARGE #17

DUKE GETS MORE CALLS THAN A MUMBAI CUSTOMER-SERVICE CENTER.

Nullus citatio.

Toss out whatever the university's current Latin motto is—probably something eloquent about creating enlightened minds via massive debt—and replace it with this one. Cast it in bronze and slap it on every brick wall and ugly, faux-Gothic building on Duke's campus.

Nullus citatio. No call.

(*Criminatio,* or "charge," should come in a close second.)

Is there another team in Division I that has led such a charmed existence when it comes to the referees? In the last decade or so, the Blue Devils have been on the friendly end of so many questionable whistles, that it's become conventional wisdom that Duke is shown favoritism like few other squads. We know it. Opposing teams know it. And most of all, Duke players know it.

Former Duke player Andre Sweet told the *Asbury Park Press* in 2003 that he's often asked whether Duke gets all the calls. "I'm like, 'Of course, it's true. It's Duke,'" he said. "It's Mike Krzyzewski. The refs were afraid of him. He could get you calls that no one else could get. That's part of playing for Duke. You know that going in."

Strange things just seem to happen when Duke takes the floor.

Foul Long Beach State.
(Courtesy of James DiBianco)

We won't bore you with an endless laundry list, but here are the greatest hits of the last few years.

In 2006, Boston College's Tyrese Rice was clobbered by Shelden Williams on a last-second drive to the basket in what would have been a game-tying bucket. *Nullus citatio.* BC lost 83–81. "I'm not going to say he did, and I'm not going to say he didn't," Rice told *The Boston Globe* of Williams's foul. "I'm just saying, look at the tape."

And while we're looking at tape, head on over to YouTube to watch the clips of Elliot Williams and Jon Scheyer basically moonwalking across the court without being whistled for traveling. *Nullus citatio.*

In 2007, the ACC was forced to publicly admit that for the second time in less than a year, Duke had won close games in

Cameron because of officiating mistakes in their favor. On January 25, Duke escaped 68–66 against Clemson after the clock operator put 4.4 seconds on the clock at the end of the game instead of the correct 1.8, allowing the Blue Devils to make the winning shot. "The league acknowledges that a timing error was made in not starting the game clock at the correct time," coordinator of officials John Clougherty later said in a statement.

A year earlier on February 4, 2006, in a game against Florida State, the refs called a head-scratching double technical on Shelden Williams and FSU's Alexander Johnson, although only Williams deserved to be T'ed. The Duke center, upset after a foul, charged Johnson, but Johnson backed away. The tech disqualified Johnson from the game. Duke went on to win in overtime, 97–96. The ACC later suspended the three officials for the mistake.

"The game's called differently on both ends of the court when you play Duke. You have the Duke rules, then you have everyone else's rules," says Bradley Vanhoy, a manager for UNC's 2005 national championship team. "It's not something you'll hear the players talk about [publicly], because they've had media training and things like that. There are certain things they can't talk about. Off the record, you'll probably find some evidence of that, but on the record, no, because [bad calls] are not something you can control in the game anyway."

"Wow, Duke is getting a lot of the calls so far!" Billy Packer famously chirped during the 2001 title game. But how to prove the favoritism? It's impossible to measure no-calls, so the best you can do is look at what is called. In other words, fouls.

In 2010–2011, Duke was 241st in the NCAA in the average number of personal fouls whistled against them—despite playing a relentless man-to-man defense whose core philosophy looks to be "all five guys foul at once." (Their number was still middle of the pack in the ACC, though.)

And then there is the foul disparity Duke has seemingly enjoyed going back to the days when the game was played with a peach basket. Over a season, the Blue Devils are consistently blown for hundreds of fewer violations than their opponents.

In 2010–2011, Duke attempted 826 free throws, while its opponents attempted 655. The year before, it was 899 to 750. In 2008–2009, 904 to 647.

During its championship run in 2000–01, the disparity was a jaw-dropping 1,001 to 701. And what's most incredible about that stat is that Duke also led the NCAA in three-point attempts for the year. How in the world does a team that's jacking so many long-range shots (as Duke does most years) also get fouled so frequently? It doesn't make any sense.

But does this prove anything? Not entirely. Most top-tier teams also enjoy a large free-throw disparity, and the refs in every conference can't be crooked, can they? No one is saying they are.

"Referees are not dishonest. They are not fixers," Len Elmore told the *Atlanta Journal-Constitution*. "Referees are human beings and, as such, susceptible to mental pressures and emotional factors, including the home crowd emotion, the subconscious desire to make up for a bad call . . . or, most significantly, the constant working over they get from coaches."

And that's where Coach K comes in. He is a master bully, riding the refs relentlessly the entire game, hurling F-bombs and generally making their lives miserable.

"That is different from other coaches," a former ACC official tells us. "If referees are doing their job, and he uses really filthy language with them, they need to let him know that when he feels like he can talk to us like he'd like for me to talk to him, then we'll talk. If he's angry or if he's trying to get an edge or whatever he's trying to do, that needs to be penalized."

"If they start getting fouls called against them, Coach K will get in the ref's ear, and as much as you'd like to believe that that doesn't make an impression, it does," says former UNC guard Dewey Burke. "They get tired of hearing from him, and few, if any, have the guts to call a T on him. Eventually they're going to listen or give Duke a call because they're tired of hearing from him. What he does works."

"With Coach K sitting on the other bench, when he stands up and gets on the referees, that's a lot of weight for the refs to carry," former Arizona guard Reggie Geary told a Tucson radio show prior to the 2011 Duke–Arizona tournament battle. "They will be starstruck."

Working the refs is hardly rare in college basketball, but what most haters object to is the frequency and nastiness in which Krzyzewski goes about his work. The former West Point cadet probably learned a little too much from his drill instructors.

There's also, like everything with Duke, the small matter of hypocrisy. For years, Coach K grumbled about North Carolina and how Dean Smith was the beneficiary of the ref's largess. Following a 1984 loss to UNC in which Coach K thought Smith should have been given a tech for banging on the scorer's table, the Duke coach unleashed one of the most famous rants in Atlantic Coast Conference basketball history.

"I want to tell you something," he snarled to the press. "When you come in here and start talking about how Duke has no class, you'd better start getting your stories straight—because our students had class and our team had class. There was not a person on our bench who was pointing a finger at the officials or banging on a scorer's table. You cannot allow people to go around pointing at officials and yelling at them without technicals being called. That is just not allowed. So, let's get some things straight around here and quit the double standard that exists in this league, all right?"

We're sure the irony of Krzyzewski's plea is not lost on anyone who's seen the coach mercilessly cuss the refs or watched his team benefit from a questionable call (like, say, three thousand charges that should have been called blocks, just picking something randomly out of the hat).

Of course, Coach K pleads the Fifth.

He told Raleigh's the *News & Observer* in 2006 that he doesn't think coaches have any effect on officiating at all. (Riiiight. Which is why he sometimes spends entire time-outs blustering at the zebras.)

"The official cannot allow that. He just can't allow that," Krzyzewski said. "He has to be influenced only by what's happening out on the court. That's why they're professionals and that's why they have to pay the price to make it to our league.

"I never look at talking to the referee as 'working' the ref," he continued. "I think that's one of the worst phrases that could ever be made. I don't think that's what happens. What you're trying to do is find out why something has been done or explain your situation. It's not a matter of 'working,' it's a matter of explanation. I don't think a really good official—and that's who we have and that's who we're going to have in the NCAA tournament—can be worked. Or else he wouldn't be in there. That's just not part of it. I think they are professionals, too."

Well, he's right about one thing, at least. It doesn't seem that the NCAA tourney refs are as susceptible to his "charms" as the regular ACC officials, who see Duke multiple times a year, often over many years. To the NCAA refs, who come from other conferences, K's foul-mouthed shtick might be unfamiliar and therefore less effective, and it doesn't take a genius to figure out that their immunity is one of the factors that bites Duke in the ass come March (along with a lack of athleticism, an overreliance on the three-ball, and so on.).

During a 2006 tourney flame-out against LSU, in which the Tigers attempted twenty-three free throws to Duke's sixteen, the Blue Devils' supposed star shooter J. J. Redick began to get frustrated.

"When he missed it, he was pretty upset," LSU's Garrett Temple said after the game. "He was complaining to the referees about not calling fouls."

For that, he'll have to wait until the conference season.

Verdict: We'll reduce this from murder to involuntary manslaughter. While the refs may not be totally in Duke's pocket, Coach K's rep and combative personality probably do earn the Devils a few more calls than opponents.

CHARGE #18

THE SCHOOL'S ARCHITECTURE SUCKS.

"You have some major issues with your foundation."

If you're a homeowner, that is the last thing you want to hear from someone inspecting your house. Those eight words could mean that you are either

1. about to be socked with a huge bill while some guys in boots and mud-stained pants dig around in the crawl space, or

2. moving out (permanently or temporarily) so that your now former abode can get a taste of a wrecking ball.

So, what does this all this Home Depot lingo have to do with Duke suckitude, you may be wondering? Are we about to tell you that the Blue Devils are responsible for the fact that you might have a quarter-inch-wide gap running along the base of your three-bedroom, two-bath McMansion?

Not exactly, but with some of Christian Laettner and Brian Davis's recent failed real estate projects, we wouldn't put it past them.

No, what we're saying is that we really hate Duke because of its architecture. Stop wrinkling your face up in incredulity. Have you ever actually walked on that campus? Have you ever actually looked at the haughty Gothic design that screams out WE ARE BETTER THAN YOU? Do you ever wonder why the hell parts of it look like they've been there since the time of Shakespeare when, in fact, the university was thrown together in the 1930s with a bunch of Lucky Strike money?

It all goes back to the guy who forked over the cash to turn Trinity College into Duke University.

We've already covered how J. B. Duke originally tried to buy Princeton before finding little ole Trinity College in rural North Carolina to take his money. And remember that J. B. Duke had an estate near Princeton and drew on that university for inspiration when creating Duke.

A few months before the official announcement of J. B. Duke's endowment in 1924, Trinity College president William Few and English professor Frank C. Brown (who was instrumental in the planning, design, and construction of the Duke campus) took a trip to several East Coast universities to gather ideas.

Guess what their major influence was.

"By far, the greatest number of notes was made at Princeton," Duke's *Library Magazine* wrote in 2005. "Few and Brown recorded information about the materials used for flooring, walls, stairwells, windows, and various other features of the buildings. In addition to notes on the buildings themselves, there are comments concerning maintenance, janitors ('All janitors men,') insurance, mail delivery, dining room and kitchen staffing, the laundry, laboratory equipment, and portraits ('Paintings of all benefactors, presidents, distinguished professors, trustees, etc.')"

Wow. Did they copy the location of every Princeton urinal, too?

But here's the best part: The architect chosen by J. B. Duke to design his namesake university was Horace Trumbauer, a man who specialized in building houses for the wealthy and had designed several of J. B. Duke's opulent residences.

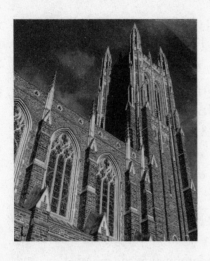

The Duke Chapel. Thanks
be to God for tobacco
money.
(Courtesy of Lee D. Baker)

At that point, Trumbauer's firm had only one academic building to its credit, the Widener Library at Harvard University—but
no matter. There's a certain beautiful symmetry to the story. How
great is that? A man who was known for designing houses for rich
people would be picked to design a university that only rich people
could afford.

But it doesn't stop there. According to Duke's own Web
site, "The arrangement of stone on Duke's older buildings was
done with the intention of making the campus look older and
more established, like its older, Northern counterparts."

Man, did J. B. Duke ever talk to a professional about this
severe case of Princeton envy? A little early-twentieth-century
electroshock might have done wonders. The guy was so desperate
to impress those back home in New Jersey, he would apparently
have gone to any length to give his upstart school the cachet of
age. He even went so far as to F up the school's building materials.

"In addition to using Gothic architecture to create an older
look, it has also been suggested that Duke's founders intentionally

placed dips in the center of buildings' steps to make it appear as though they had been walked upon for centuries," *The Chronicle* wrote in 2011. "Timothy Pyatt, Duke University Archivist, noted that although it is clear the steps could not have naturally become as worn as they are in the short time since their construction in 1930, there is nothing in the University documentation that confirms the steps were intentionally built to look weather-beaten."

Come again? So everyone agrees that the steps were clearly faked but no one can find the evidence? What happened here? Did Colonel Nathan R. Jessup from *A Few Good Men* doctor the flight log? Or maybe Coach K cursed some poor archivist for two hours straight until that information "disappeared"?

Whatever happened, the conclusion is the same. Duke is a big phony. It is a lie built atop a fib laid atop a feint. It is nothing but a grand deception. The very foundation of the university, the actual buildings themselves, were designed to look like something they are not. The entire school was borne out of chasing someplace better, something more revered, someplace prettier.

Is it any wonder then that the Cameron Crazies are so insufferably arrogant? Is it any wonder that every Duke player is convinced that he's never actually committed a foul in a basketball game? Is it any wonder that K's hair is jet-black in color even though he's eligible for AARP membership?

Jesus H., the very buildings that they see every day on their way to class, practice and weekly blood-draining sessions (we're convinced Coach K is a vampire, FYI) reinforce the notion that they are more important than those around them. The bricks and stones continuously perpetrate a myth to these assholes that they are part of something that they are, in fact, not.

Duke is no more Princeton than DisneyWorld's Space Mountain is an actual mountain. And no amount of faux-Gothic crap and preworn granite steps will ever change that.

Verdict: Bulldoze every building. Burn the land to replenish the soil. Put in another SuperMegaGigante Walmart. At least that's honest about what it is.

EXHIBIT G

THE ELTON BRAND E-MAIL

Elton Brand may be an overpaid, underachieving lug in the pros, but we love the guy. In fact, he may be our all-time, number-one favorite Dookie. (In fairness, that list is not long.) It all goes back to the infamous 1999 e-mail he sent to a snotty Duke alum who questioned his decision to bolt for the NBA after his sophomore year. The exchange is annotated below for your reading pleasure.

From: Taylor, Jennifer
Sent: Friday, April 16, 1999 2:55 PM **[Note: written during office hours]**
To: Brand, Elton
Subject: Leaving Duke

I graduated from Duke last May and just wanted to express my disgust for your decision to leave the Duke program after only two years. **[You totally should have stayed and gotten a worthless sociology degree, like the other ball players.]** As an alum, not only do I hold the school in high regard, but the basketball program as well **[After the national championship, I got drunk and painted my chest blue.]**, especially since both have deservedly garnered such a great deal of respect for their accomplishments.

As part of our basketball program, you represent Duke as a whole. We are first and foremost an academic school **[despite all the spelling and grammar errors in this e-mail]**, you clearly did not belong at Duke in the first place if this was the extent of your commitment to Duke and a college education in general. You have not only insulted the current students who are putting in four years at a school they love **[but have no jump shot whatsoever]**, but also the thousands of alumni who have realized the value of a Duke education and what an honor and privilege it was to be there for four years **[at a cost of $200,000, hardly a financial burden at all]**.

If you do not realize the opportunity you has infront of you to play for Coach K and at the same time attain a Duke diploma, then that is certainly your loss **[never mind the $3.4 million you'll make your first year in the NBA]**. I just wish that you has spared us the notion that you were continuing in the tradition of being a Duke student-athlete, in emphasizing excellence in both academics and athletics **[like the lacrosse team]**. You will not be considered part of the Duke family, in my mind as well as many others. You have by no means proved yourself worthy of that title.

Sincerely,
Jennifer Taylor **[Damn, I hope this email never gets out.]**

DUKE SUCKS

From: Elton Tyron Brand
Sent: Sunday, April 25, 1999 8:05 PM
To: Taylor, Jennifer
Subject: Re: Leaving Duke

Thank you very much, for reminding me of the reason why
I left Duke. [**Also, Durham is kind of a hellhole. Seriously, have you been there? Have you?**] People like you
can not and will not ever understand my situation. I'm sure
daddy worked very hard to send your rich self to college.
While real people struggle. [**Like my teammate Chris Car-
rawell. You think that dude is ever gonna make ends
meet in the league?**] I would also like to extend an invita-
tion for you not to waste your or my time ever agin. Never
being considered a part of your posh group of yuppies really hurts me to the heart. Yeah, right. Because I don't care
about you or your alumni.

Sincerely, [**Or should I close with "love?"**]
Elton Brand #42 NBA

CHARGE #19

DUKE PLAYERS IN THE NBA ARE NOT EXACTLY SETTING THE WORLD ON FIRE.

As North Carolina grads, we consistently root against Duke. We have trouble really enjoying the NCAA Tournament until Duke goes out in its usual early-round blaze of glory. And when Coach K sat on the bench for the USA National Basketball team (we can't really call that job "coaching" or "leading"), we'll admit under threat of deportation that we pulled for Greece. And maybe Spain. What can we say? We're suckers for floppy hair.

When it comes to the NBA playoffs, we align our rooting interests around whoever has the least number of former Blue Devils on their teams (with zero being the optimal number).

In this case, though, we usually have nothing to worry about. For all of the stars Duke has had in college, the lack of success that these alumni have had in the NBA playoffs is stunning. It's like a mirror image of what happens to them in college: puff up the numbers during the regular season and choke like a dog that drinks his water too fast in the postseason.

Let's look at the stat of "win shares," from 1976–77 through the 2009–2010 seasons. The win shares formula is complicated—it includes number of possessions for each player, marginal offense, and other numbers—but the basic idea is to measure how much an individual player contributes to his team's wins or losses.

We broke this stat down by where the players went to college

Carlos Boozer reflects on
why he fell to the second
round.
(Courtesy of Keith Allison)

(if they did). Duke actually comes out third overall behind UNC
and UCLA, respectively, in terms of regular-season win shares.
That means former Duke players do actually contribute to NBA
regular-season wins. (We were as surprised as you are.)

But when you get into the playoffs, the bottom drops out.

In playoff win shares, the Blue Devils tumble all the way
down to twenty-fourth, behind such powerhouse NBA factories
as Clemson, Minnesota, and Virginia Union. (UNC and UCLA
remain first and second in playoff win shares.)

And it gets even worse. When you compare the ratio of playoff wins to regular-season wins, you have to go all the way down
to number sixty-four Oklahoma to find a college with a propor-
tionally worse amount of playoff success than Duke.

More appalling yet, if you look at the 117 colleges that have
at least five players with NBA win shares in the 1977–2010 time

frame, Duke ranks ninety-third in terms of proportional playoff success.

That's pathetic. Over this same time period, take a guess at how many former Duke players have won NBA championship rings. The number is one, the loneliest number. Danny Ferry "earned" his as a benchwarmer for the San Antonio Spurs in 2003.

And this is a university that in the last decade alone has produced eight first-round picks: Gerald Henderson, J. J. Redick, Shelden Williams, Luol Deng, Dahntay Jones, Jason Williams, Mike Dunleavy, and Shane Battier. None has had even the faintest sniff of a ring.

But being a blue-chipper doesn't necessarily guarantee success if you're coming out of Duke. The school's McDonald's All-Americans have fared much worse in the NBA than those from other schools. From 2001–2007, just 5.9 percent of Duke's Mickey D's boys wound up as NBA starters, compared to 18.2 percent from other schools. "Which begs the question," *Sports Illustrated* wrote, "did Duke recruit these players because they were good enough to be McDonald's All-Americans, or did many of them become McDonald's All-Americans simply because Duke was recruiting them?"

Another analysis of Duke suckitude in the pros comes courtesy of stats master Roland Beech of 82games.com. Beech studied the performance of each college's draft picks from 1989–2009. He compared their output with an expected rating: a weighted average of (points + rebounds + assists / game) determined by a school's distribution of draft positions.

What the numbers show is that of the twenty-three colleges with twelve or more picks from 1989–2008, only Indiana (led by Coach K's mentor, Bob Knight, for over half the years in this time frame) produced more underachieving (relative to draft position) pros than Duke. UConn pros, for example, perform a bit better than expected. North Carolina's pros performed exactly as well as expected based on average draft position. Of course, the 1989 starting point used by Beech fails to include the distinguished pro careers of such Tar Heels legends as Michael Jordan, James Worthy, Bob McAdoo, Billy Cunningham, Walter Davis, Bobby Jones, and Brad Daugherty. Coach K loses the considerably less stellar group of Johnny Dawkins, Mark Alarie, David Henderson, and Martin Nessley from his pre-1989 years.

The moral of the story? Coach K may be in the basketball hall of fame, but none of his players is. And if they keep playing like they have in the NBA postseason, it's gonna stay that way.

Verdict: If you are hanging your hat on the ass-end of Danny Ferry's career, you are guilty.

CHARGE #20

DUKE FLOPS WORSE THAN A LATTER-DAY NIC CAGE MOVIE.

Forget about a national championship. The trophy Duke players seem most intent on winning is an Oscar. We've seen less convincing acting in a summer stock production of *Our Town*.

We're talking about the flop, one of the lamest and yet most effective weapons in Duke's arsenal. These guys spend more time on their backs than porn stars. Watch in amazement as Greg Paulus gets thrown backward by the merest brush of an elbow. Watch as Shane Battier gets tossed into Row B by the stiff wind created as a better player blows by him. Watch Kyle Singler get knocked nearly unconscious after the guy he's defending dares to gently turn around while holding the basketball.

Shane Battier in a rare moment of standing upright. *(Courtesy of Keith Allison)*

Sorry, is this college hoops or a game in the second-division Italian soccer league?

We understand there will probably always be need to make certain a ref sees it when you take a charge. We get that the block/charge decision is one of the toughest a ref has to make. But what Duke has done to push the envelope on drawing bogus calls is absurd. The team is so consistent year to year that at some point you have to ask yourself, "Is there some sort of instructional video that's mailed to every Duke recruit prior to his freshman year?" How could player after player deploy the same cheap tactics if they weren't being institutionalized in some way?

"This is the decade in which the word 'flop' became synonymous with Duke hoopsters' overzealous attempts to draw offensive fouls," wrote *Sports Illustrated* of the 2000s.

"I don't know if because people have talked about it so much that they've bought into [flopping], but they're doing it more and more now," says former UNC guard Bobby Frasor. "The flopping—I don't know what they do in practice. They must teach something on taking an exorbitant amount of charges. If you look at YouTube and look at Duke flopping, there are so many funny videos on there. It is reality."

It goes beyond the videos, Bobby. There is even a Duke Flops Drinking Game. The rules are simple: You basically take a drink every time a Duke player flops. This is a terrific way to kick off a weekend bender, but it will occasionally lead to alcohol-induced death.

"There's no question that they try to buy offensive charges by the way they flop around," says former UNC guard Dewey

Burke. "Refs are more likely to give someone a call when a player puts his body on the line.

"We never talked about them actually practicing it, but they must. They must at least discuss it, because it's been pretty consistent," Burke says. "I can't imagine there's a drill designed to work on that, but I think they definitely talk about it. When a guy is penetrating hard, and it's obvious there's going to be contact, as soon as there's contact, they just fall down. Any time anybody drives and someone steps over, they're gonna try and take a charge and just fall down."

"Do we use it as a tactic? Absolutely," Duke forward Gerald Henderson admitted to the Raleigh *News & Observer* in 2008. "We're a team that's not going to be able to block a whole lot of shots. If we do [block shots], it'll be from the help side and a lot of perimeter blocked shots. So we have to be quick and help each other inside by getting into position [for charges].

"You gotta sell the call," Henderson said, grinning. "I don't have a percentage for you. You have to sell it to the referee."

Or how about this blatant admission by Sir Floppier himself, Shane Battier? Dan Patrick of *Sports Illustrated* asked Battier if, while looking back at his college days, he is on "the Mount Rushmore of taking fake charges"?

"I only faked half the time," Battier said in the 2011 interview. "I always said that the ability to draw the charge was essential to my career. People didn't know if I was going to jump out of the way, if I was going to dive under them, if I was going to block their shot."

Sir Floppier's strategy, however, may be backfiring for Duke.

"I think they've gotten less of those calls the last couple of years, because the officials have gotten wise to it," Burke says. "Four, five, six years ago, it was ridiculous. Refs are getting wise to it, but also the opposing coach is going to say to the refs, 'Watch for the flops. They flop nearly every time we penetrate.'"

"Eventually, the actors hurt themselves because as many teams as we have, [the officials] get to know who are the guys who are trying to fool them, and they discuss those things in the pregame—the certain players out there that are taking flops, not contact," John Clougherty, the ACC officials coordinator, told the *News & Observer*.

Sure to further hamper Duke's antics is the charge circle, first instituted in the 2011–2012 season, that defines how close to the basket a defender can be in order to draw a call.

"I'm waiting for them to put in the [half circle] to take that flop stuff out," says former UNC forward Jackie Manuel. "I mean, that's what [Duke] works on and they're really good at it. You can't hate on them because it's part of the game. I don't like it but it's part of it."

But Duke and its bench-full of Oliviers is far from beaten. Even with the half circle and the refs getting wise to their tricks, the Blue Devils will surely continue to innovate. Take J. J. Redick, who was probably not the inventor of the radical "offensive flop," but he was surely one of its most skilled practitioners. Redick's flop involved wildly kicking out his legs as he went up for a jump shot, making it appear that contact was made by a defender. (Again, check the YouTube evidence. It's priceless.) After Redick had moved on from Duke, Jon Scheyer became the reigning master of this lame new move.

The point is that these tricks, like Native-American stories or the human papillomavirus, will never go away because they continue to be passed down from generation to generation. Duke will always be the first, last and next name in flops, because they were evidently born without the shame gene.

During a 2008 exhibition game against Lenoir-Rhyne in Cameron, senior Josh Rudder, who was guarding Jon Scheyer, suddenly fell to the floor in an attempt to draw an offensive foul.

"I've been watching them forever," Rudder, who grew up a Duke fan, later told the *Burlington Times-News*. "I learned it from them."

The flop may be occasionally effective, but who besides Coach K is willing to win that way? Not other coaches in the conference.

"I hate teams that just flop all the time, and if you see one of my guys flopping, then it's a guy that I'm going to be really ticked at," UNC coach Roy Williams told the *News & Observer*. "Twenty years as a head coach and I've never had anybody that other teams would talk about as a flopper."

"I'll never forget one practice when someone flopped, and Coach Williams stopped practice, and he said, 'Hey! We are not going to play that way. We will never.' He was very stern about it," Burke recalls. "He didn't even have to say anything about Duke. We knew what he meant."

Verdict: With so much unimpeachable video evidence floating around, it's hard to argue that flopping strategies, if not outright taught, are handed down from player to player. Duke is sentenced to time served plus a half circle painted under the basket.

CHARGE #21

THE CAMERON CRAZIES AIN'T ALL THEY'RE CRACKED UP TO BE. CLAP, CLAP, CLAP-CLAP-CLAP.

Before they were known as the Cameron Crazies, they were called the Student Animals. And "Animals" was right. Rarely had college basketball seen such a rowdy, obnoxious, and downright rude crowd in any arena. These Dookies may have been geniuses in the classroom, but when they set foot in Cameron, they acted like a pack of wild hyenas hopped up on feline pheromones, ready to take down the other team by any means necessary.

These were fans who taunted. They cursed. They threw things and generally made asses of themselves. They probably ate raw meat and pooped in the quad.

During the first national telecast from Cameron in 1979, NBC insisted on a time-delay so the raucous fans could be censored if necessary.

So screw all this "Cameron Crazy" business. That's too soft a nickname. It's too laudatory. Let's start a movement, right here and now, to go back to calling these Duke fans what they are: "Animals." From here on out, no more "Crazies," only "Animals."

But no matter what we call them, it's unlikely to improve their image. No one seems to like the Animals much, except the Animals themselves. And Dick Vitale, of course. A 1996 poll conducted by North Carolina's *News & Record* anointed Duke fans the most obnoxious with a landslide 52 percent. (UNC was

Cameron originally cost $400,000 to build—lunch money for current students. *(Courtesy of Lesley Looper)*

second at 27 percent.) "You can't stand to be there, even if you're pulling for Duke," one reader wrote. "Who else can it be," wrote another, "but the University of New Jersey at Durham? They need to grow up."

Good luck with that, especially if the Animals continue to get the endless praise from those who cover college basketball as the best crowd in basketball or generally anywhere on planet earth. Fans in arenas, such as Illinois, Kansas, Clemson, and the University of New Mexico should stage a sit-in protest in Coach K's office—if he didn't have a fingerprint scanner protecting it.

So, let's take a closer look at the Animals and some of the myths that continually are attached to them.

MYTH #1: THEY ARE FUNNY.

Hmmm. Humor is in the eye of the beholder, but better words to describe the Animals might be "crude" and "mean-spirited." The list of offenses they have committed against opposing players is longer than the number of useless McDonald's All-Americans on Coach K's bench laid end to end.

Georgia Tech's Dennis Scott, who was a bit on the heavy side, was showered with Twinkies. The Animals made fun of North Carolina guard Steve Hale, who had recently suffered a collapsed lung, with chants of "inhale" and "exhale." The Animals hurled pizza boxes at NC State's Lorenzo Charles after he was arrested for beating up a pizza delivery guy. And on and on.

"We talk about role models, about coaches and players being role models," Dean Smith said back in 1996 after the Animals had yelled crude taunts at UNC guard Jeff McInnis. "How about Duke students? I think they should be role models, too. The esteemed Duke faculty has to be embarrassed. That's ridiculous. I think the schools have to do something. The ACC office has to do something. It won't happen here [in Chapel Hill]."

Ha? Anyone laughing?

The most infamous incident occurred in 1984 when Maryland visited Cameron. Terrapins guard Herman Veal had been investigated for sexual battery, so the Animals chanted "R-A-P-E," and threw hundreds of condoms on the court during the pregame warm-up. The stunt forced Duke president Terry Sanford to pen an open letter to the students, pleading with them to shape up.

"I don't think we need to be crude and obscene to be effectively enthusiastic," Sanford wrote. "We can cheer and taunt with style; that should be the Duke trademark. Crudeness, profanity, and cheapness should not be our reputation—but it is . . . I hope you will discipline yourselves and your fellow students. This request is in keeping with my commitment to self-government for students. It should not be up to me to enforce proper behavior that signifies the intelligence of Duke students. You should do it. Reprove those who make us all look bad. Shape up your own language. I hate for us to have the reputation of being stupid."

MYTH #2: THEY ARE CREATIVE GENIUSES.

Not hardly. What seems spontaneous on television is actually carefully planned and choreographed through the students' cheer sheets—a catalog of potential chants prepared by the line monitors and distributed before games. When Maryland came to town in 2009, a cheer-sheet item read, "Gary Williams tends to sweat. A LOT. Make liberal use of 'Sweat, Gary, sweat!' when he gets nervous." For Roy Williams, who suffers from vertigo, the cheer sheet suggested, "Roy is diz-zy. Clap, clap, clap-clap-clap."

"When I was in school, the students were great and the team was bad. Now it's the other way around," college basketball author and Duke alumnus John Feinstein told the *News & Observer* in 2009.

Duke historian Bill Brill thinks the Crazies—sorry, the Animals—no longer display the same spontaneity as they did in the late 1970s. "I hear that [complaint] all the time," he told the *News & Observer*. "I think in a sense they're right, because it's so much more orchestrated today. But that's all television-driven, from my perspective."

True enough. It's difficult to shake the feeling that so much of what the student section does is in service of the TV cameras. Cameron even has two sides: the so-called TV side and the non-TV side. Students are acutely aware of which side is which, and they scratch and claw to get on the TV side. Meanwhile, anyone who's ever attended a game at Cameron knows the non-TV side is a lot less rowdy.

Sports Illustrated spoke to some devoted Duke fans in 1986 who were covering themselves in royal-blue paint. Was this ritual "designed to psych them up, to fulfill some remnant primal urge?" the writer asked. "Nah," one student replied, "We want to get on TV."

A Duke student called out the obnoxious Crazies in a 2004 student-newspaper editorial, writing, "You suck," and calling them "phony, little nerds." *(Courtesy of Brian Allen)*

MYTH #3: THEY ARE EFFECTIVE.

This is probably the biggest and most widely perpetrated misconception that there is. Besides their desire to get on TV, the Animals cheer, stomp, and scream inappropriate things at rival players because they believe it's helping their team. Coach K and every sportscaster on the planet has talks about how helpful the crowd is, and the Animals are known as Duke's "sixth man," so it must be true.

"The Duke University student section with their clever taunts and Speedo attire? Despite Coach K's insistence to the contrary, they don't, sad to say, have much impact on the players," wrote Tobias J. Moskowitz and L. Jon Wertheim in their book *Scorecasting: The Hidden Influences Behind How Sports Are Played and Games Are Won.*

The authors examined the one stat they felt could be affected by the crowd, free-throw shooting, and found that over the last two decades in the NBA, teams have shot exactly the same percentage on the road as at home.

If you look at shooting in Cameron specifically over the 2009–2011 seasons, for example, you also don't find much evidence that the crowd is significantly shifting things in the Blue Devils' favor. Here's what we found. During the 2010–2011 season, Duke hosted seventeen games at Cameron. In those games, ten opponents shot a lower percentage than they did for the season as a whole and seven teams shot better. For the 2009–2010 season, nine opponents shot worse and eight opponents shot better. The data are pretty much inconclusive.

In other words, all those blue-painted assholes aren't really doing much except clogging their pores.

"A lot of times," Duke's Shelden Williams told the *News & Record* in 2005, "I don't even know what they're saying."

"It wasn't really loud at all," says former UNC guard Daniel Bolick of a 2011 game at Cameron. "And I thought with all this hype around the Cameron Crazies, I expected a little more. They didn't really pump the crowd up when Duke was playing poorly. But really most of the sound comes from the fact that it's a small gym and it echoes well. But as far as the Crazies go, there were a few signs but I don't see much of a difference between Cameron and a place like Florida or Pittsburgh that has students all around the court. The biggest difference is that the venue is smaller so the sound echoes more than anything."

"I think one year, my freshman year, just going into that environment for the first time, I was a little nervous and it showed in the first five minutes," says former UNC forward Jackie Manuel. "But I enjoy it, because I look at it as a high-school atmosphere. Ever since then I enjoyed playing there. They didn't bother me at all after that."

And as UConn's Geno Auriemma pointed out, perhaps the Animals shouldn't exactly be taking credit for what goes on in Cameron. "As far as the Cameron Crazies are concerned, I think they're a little bit overrated," he told the *News & Observer* in 2003. "I don't think the Cameron Crazies would be as effective if the Duke basketball players weren't as good."

In the Animals' defense, they at least no longer have the rep of being the most uncouth fans in the game.

"They are not crude there," says former UNC guard Dewey Burke. "They have jokes and chant stuff, but they're not crude. NC State and Maryland fans will say some of the most awful things you've ever heard. I mean racist or family-oriented. It really crosses the line. You hear that and you step back and say, 'Really?'"

Verdict: Maryland and NC State are probably dirtier, but the Cameron Animals definitely don't deserve their rep as the best fans on the planet. Can't we all just move on?

CHARGE #22

DUKE IS MOST HATED IN ITS OWN BACKYARD.

We've well established that Duke is the most hated team on planet Earth. And probably on other planets, though we admit, we haven't exactly checked. Think about that for a minute. It's entirely possible that right this second some alien civilization in a faraway solar system is for the first time receiving television transmissions of the 1992 Duke–Kentucky game that have been traveling for decades through the vacuum of space, and these alien viewers are turning to each other and asking in a strange, telepathic language, "What's with this douche, Christian Laettner?"

But aliens be damned. They never know what they're talking about, except when it comes to quark drives and anal probes. Duke must have its share of fans, especially in their home state of North Carolina, right?

Ehhhh, not so much.

A Public Policy poll conducted leading up to the UNC–Duke matchup in February 2010 found that in the state of North Carolina, almost twice as many of respondents would be pulling for North Carolina as for those guys eight miles down the road.

This pathetic, stepchild existence is hardly news to Duke players. "In Durham there are Duke fans, but once you get outside the area, there are a lot of Carolina fans and NC State fans," Duke forward Kyle Singler told the *Indianapolis Star* in 2010. "North Carolina as a state is not a Duke-friendly state."

In other words, Durham is like some sort of Soweto ghetto, where the minority Duke fans live oppressed and cowed existences behind six-foot stone walls, waiting for that terrible day when a redneck state fan will show up with firearms and demand their land and late-model BMWs.

But at least they're loved in their home city of Durham, right? The town must throw the team a grand ticker-tape parade attended by tens of thousands when Duke brings home the Wooden Trophy.

Wrong again. Following its most recent national championship in 2010, the team was treated to a modest celebration held in downtown Durham beneath a water tower painted with the Lucky Strike logo. Just one thousand people showed up. (In contrast, some 40,000 lined Hartford's streets to cheer UConn after the 2011 championship.) To make matters worse, Duke was forced to share the fete with the Durham Bulls, the local baseball team who had won the minor-league crown the previous season. An hour after the piddling Duke celebration, more than nine thousand locals turned out to support the Bulls for their home opener, which was being played . . . in a stadium directly across the street.

Oh, the humanity.

Maybe Singler should have been a little more specific. It does seem that Durham is home to plenty of Duke fans—as long as you don't count the parts of Durham outside of the Duke campus.

Take a look at the photo on the next page, snapped in summer 2011 at a national sporting goods chain less than thirty minutes outside of Durham. That's thousands of dollars of Duke merchandise gathering dust on the clearance rack.

And just to be clear, we did not go looking for this photo. We

Taken less than twenty miles from Duke's campus.

did not travel from store to store for weeks until we found two shipping containers' worth of royal-blue merchandise marked down. If you live in North Carolina, you happen upon this pathetic reality all the time.

On the next page is another photo taken at a different chain in Apex, North Carolina (about thirty miles from the Duke campus), taken in October 2010.

It's typical of all of the local racks. UNC stuff is nearly sold out. Even the NC State racks have a dent in them. The Duke items are collecting dust. They can't give the stuff away. The factories may as well just deliver the goods straight to the landfills.

On page 148, you'll find another photo from summer 2011. It's from a Raleigh-area Build-A-Bear workshop. (Don't ask what we were doing there. It had something to do with national security.) The store offers a selection of Duke and UNC outfits in which children can dress their teddy bear. Look closely at those racks.

Taken in Durham, North Carolina. No lie.

The Duke one is completely full. No takers. Even children—as sweet and naïve and impressionable and unworldly as they are—have already learned to hate the Blue Devils. We've never been prouder of youngsters in the state of North Carolina.

Though to be fair, Duke doesn't seem to be selling much anywhere else, either. The school ranked thirty-eighth in merchandise sales, according to the October–December 2010 figures (the most recent at press time) released by the Collegiate Licensing Company.

(Even Clemson sold enough scratch to sneak in at twenty-fifth, although the Tigers haven't done anything significant in major sports since Danny Ford beat Tom Osborne's Nebraska Cornhuskers in the 1981 Orange Bowl for the title. But we're guessing they didn't hold on at twenty-five because of people hunting down that orange number 7 Cliff Austin jersey.)

The most damning point of all is that Duke didn't even crack the Top 25 for the 2009–10 fiscal year, even though sales were

Taken less than a year after Duke's national championship.

measured through June 30, 2010—as in some three months after Duke beat Butler to capture the national title. Crowns are supposed to earn schools new fans or send current fans running to the store to load up on licensed mugs, T-shirts, and sweatpants with the name of the school slapped across the ass. (We still don't understand that fashion trend.) In the same year, Alabama jumped from fifth to second place on the list specifically on the strength of its football championship. Duke got no similar bump.

In fact, they're actually getting *less* popular, if that's even possible. In 2008–09, the Blue Devils ranked thirty-third in sales.

But it's not all gloom and doom for the Blue Devils. There is one place in America where Duke is beloved, where Kyle Singler is actually thought to be deserving of preseason All-American honors, where Bobby Hurley is not treated like something sticky you scrape off your boot. If you guessed New Jersey, give yourself a cookie.

"Duke is absolutely huge there," Duke big man Brian Zoubek, a Jersey native (aren't they all?) told the *Indianapolis Star* in 2010. "North Carolina is big, but not as big as Duke.

"But when you get down there, it's UNC, UNC, UNC, and some NC State," he rants. "There's a little bit of a Duke following, but nothing compared to the North Carolina following. We're used to being the hated ones."

No wonder Duke is known as the University of New Jersey at Durham. It all makes sense now. Hated state, hated school. Bingo. The two just go together.

But here's an odd thought. Despite its rep for producing annoying gangsters and more annoying reality-show cast members, New Jersey isn't actually all that bad. It's got some beautiful landscapes and beaches, and most of its people are pretty decent. We've been there.

So, what if the problem is not that Duke is being dragged down by New Jersey, but precisely the opposite? That Jersey's rep has been destroyed by becoming so closely linked to Duke? The school is like some fungus that has attached itself to the very image of the state.

For the sake of its future and its children, Jersey needs to fight back. Rise up, Trenton! Rise up, Atlantic City! Vanquish the stench of the Dookies from your hallowed gardens and rest stops! It's not too late!

You must become like the citizens of North Carolina and reject everything that has to do with the Blue Devils. Maybe then, everyone will stop joking about how bad your state smells.

Verdict: Guilty of local hatred. The next time Duke wins something of significance, they better fly in to Raleigh-Durham airport in an unmarked plane. Or at least make a connection in Newark first.

CHARGE #23

COACH K IS TOO GOOD TO AUTOGRAPH ANYTHING FOR YOU.

It's true. It says it right there on his official Web site. "Coach K is not able to honor autograph requests at this time."

Seriously, Coach K? Anyone who says they're too busy or important to take out a pen and scribble his name had better be literally a few minutes away from curing cancer. Even the leader of the free world, Barack Obama, and America's own female Jesus, Oprah, aren't above sending signed photos to admirers.

Are you, Coach K, saying that you are more important than Obama or Oprah? Are you saying that you are busier? Obama is occupied managing two wars and trying to contain a nuclear Iran. You are teaching young men how to throw a ball into a peach basket and searching for the correct shade of Just For Men.

Granted, when your last name has two of every letter in the alphabet, autographs can be a bit of a hardship, but still. How long can it realistically take to sign something, Coach K? Two seconds? Three seconds tops? Even if you signed a hundred photos a day, every single day, that would still only add up to a half hour of work a week.

You spend more time yelling the F-word.

But even if you are too busy, Coach K, you could always get some of your freshmen to help out. Think of it as one of your beloved hazing rituals. A player misses a foul shot at practice, and as punishment, he'll be forced to run a lap, then forge your signature on a letter.

DUKE SUCKS

Everyone wins. Well, except for the player and the person receiving the letter.

But at least your precious hands are spared from the inevitable carpal tunnel and will remain healthy enough for years to come to do what they were intended to do: point your middle finger skyward at the refs.

Verdict: Guilty. It's hard to say what is worse: Coach K's attitude or his penmanship.

EXHIBIT H

WHY YOUR TEAM HATES DUKE

For fans of many schools, there is usually that one horrible, crystallizing moment—be it during a chance meeting in the NCAA Tournament or some regular-season matchup—when their team gets unfairly punked by the Devils, and they suddenly find themselves among the very swollen ranks of Duke enemies. It happens to many. And if it hasn't happened to your team yet, just wait. There is surely a postseason debacle in your future. Here now, is a list of the exact moment your team got Dookied.

School: University of Kentucky
Date: March 29, 1992
Scene of the crime: Philadelphia, PA
The smoking gun: The Stomp. Which preceded "the shot."
'Nuf said.

School: Indiana University
Date: April 4, 1992
Scene of the crime: Minneapolis, MN
The smoking gun: Up by double digits in the first half, Indiana watches as three of their top players (Damon Bailey, Calbert Cheaney, and Greg Graham) foul out in the second half, leading to a 31–6 Duke run. Just FYI, Bailey averaged about two fouls per game for his career. Chaney averaged 2.5. Graham averaged under 2.

School: Clemson University

Date: January 25, 2007

Scene of the crime: Cameron Indoor Stadium

The smoking gun: With five seconds left and Duke up by three, the Devils throw away the inbounds pass to Clemson's Vernon Hamilton, who gathers himself and nails a three to tie the game. In reality, the play took about 2.2 seconds to happen, but somehow, magically, Duke is given 4.4 seconds at the end of the game instead of 2.8 and consequently makes a game-winning layup with .1 second left. In a statement released later, John Clougherty, ACC supervisor of officials, said it was a "timing error."

School: University of Maryland

Date: March 31, 2001

Scene of the crime: Minneapolis, MN—The Final Four

The Smoking gun: The Terrapins and Devils already had a long-standing, nasty rivalry, but when an injustice during a game of this magnitude comes along, it takes the hatred up a few notches. We'll let Bill Berghel of *The Sports Report* take it from here. "The one last week, Duke–Maryland. I sometimes play a little game where I count unfair calls for each side," he wrote. "I rarely see a difference of more than six. In this game, I counted a 24–4 Duke advantage (and that includes the bizarre charging foul against Shane Battier). Maryland could have been UCLA in the early 1970s, and it wouldn't have made a difference. Of course, Jim Nance and Billy Packer, both massive Duke fans, hardly mentioned it. But the fans were aware of it. Watch the replays of Duke on offense, and especially Battier. I counted no fewer than twelve uncalled charges against the Blue Devils, charges where the exact same thing was called against Maryland. Fairleigh-Dickinson could have won with that kind of officiating. I now believe this to be the worst-officiated game I've ever seen. And somebody has a lot of explaining to do."

School: The University of Arizona
Date: April 2, 2001
Scene of the crime: Minneapolis, MN—The National Championship Game
The smoking gun: Star Duke guard Jason Williams finishes with only four fouls even though several in the national media questioned no-calls throughout the game.

School: Baylor University
Date: March 28, 2010
Scene of the crime: Houston, TX—Regional Final
The smoking gun: With 4:37 to go and Baylor up 59–57, Bears forward Quincy Acy drives baseline and collides with Duke's seven-foot center Brian Zoubek. Only Acy gets called for a charge. Duke hits a three-pointer on the next possession for a five-point swing and a 60–59 lead, on their way to a 78–71 win. "That was a lucky blow of the whistle," Monchichi-lookalike Zoubek would later say.

School: Butler University
Date: April 5, 2010
Scene of the crime: Indianapolis, IN—National Championship
The smoking gun: Up by one with less than a minute to go in the game, Duke's Kyle Singler bricks a shot. Under the

basket, Brian Zoubek throws Butler's Matt Howard to the ground in a battle for the rebound. No call. Even though the Bulldogs got the ball out of bounds from the scrum, the play should have been Zoubek's fifth foul, which would have sent 80 percent free-throw shooter Matt Howard to the line for two shots. Butler loses 61–59.

CHARGE #24

COACH K'S PROGRAM HAS HAD MORE DEFECTORS THAN CUBA.

If there were a twelve-step program for players bolting, Coach K would right now be standing in a church basement somewhere and quietly admitting to a group of strangers over punch, "My name is Mike, and I have a transfer problem."

Over the years, more players have deserted Duke than wives from Larry King. It's almost like Duke's own players hate it as much as the rest of us do.

(Then again, have you been to Durham? You wouldn't stay, either.)

Players abandon the Duke basketball program at such an alarming rate that Coach K has had more McDonald's All-Americans leave the program than Clemson has recruited. Ever. You don't see that banner hanging in Cameron.

Bill Jackman left in 1983 after his freshman year. Greg Wendt left in 1983 after his sophomore year. Crawford Palmer and Billy McCaffrey both bolted in 1991.

Christian Ast, Mike Chappell, Chris Burgess, Andre Sweet, Eric Boateng, Taylor King, Elliot Williams also peaced out, and the list goes on and on.

Jamal Boykin (2006) and Michael Thompson (2003) couldn't even stomach finishing out the year, and left midseason.

In 2009, Olek Czyz marked the fifth transfer in four years.

And this isn't even counting the other players who left early under the guise of "turning pro early." Josh McRoberts came to

Duke as a McDonald's All-American and the number one recruit in the land, but never lived up to the hype. After his junior year and with no hope of improving his stock, he declared early for the NBA draft, despite having no chance of going in the first round and securing a guaranteed contract.

McRoberts ended up as a second-round pick and continues his undistinguished play for the Pacers. Maybe he should have declared for the WNBA draft instead.

Shavlik Randolph also came to Duke as a McDonald's All-American and Top 10 recruit. After three years of disappointing play during which he asserted himself mostly by fouling at a historic clip, he declared early for the draft.

Randolph went undrafted, but eventually glommed on to a roster spot in Philadelphia, whose general manager just happened to be Duke alum Billy King. Funny that.

He's just another in a long line of curious defections.

But how can that be? Isn't Duke supposed to be the premier program in the country, its coach the most inspiring leader since Churchill? (That was certainly the takeaway from Coach K's self-serving Chevy commercial.)

So why are so many young players running from the university like it was a warehouse fire?

The answer is probably a mix of things—none of them good.

One issue is certainly playing time. Heralded recruits who were top dogs in high school come in expecting to start, and then end up getting pushed out by more talented players.

But there seems to be more to it than that. One popular theory is that the high transfer rate is about Coach K cleansing the program of his recruiting mistakes. A player comes in and doesn't live up to the coach's expectations, so instead of having the player eat up four years' worth of scholarships, Coach K simply nudges them out the door. So much for loyalty.

Bill Jackman, a highly touted forward who arrived in Durham for the 1982–1983 season, left after a single year. Legend has it, after being ordered to play in the post during practice, he looked at Jay Bilas, Mark Alarie, and the team's other big men and replied, "Gee, Coach, there are some big boys down there."

Who wouldn't want to be rid of that dead weight?

With a couple of exceptions, most of the players who leave Duke have been disappointments. It's not hard to imagine the hard-assed Coach K making their life hell until they decide that Duke is not for them.

Center Chris Burgess departed in 1999, following gripes about playing time and clashes between his father and Coach K.

"He's petty and dishonest," Burgess's father said of Coach K. "If you aren't on his good side, he doesn't fix that. If you are, you can do no wrong. It's like Shane Battier—he can't do anything wrong. [Coach K] has no sons, and he picks one of the boys to be his son, and he can do no wrong. Even the players on the team called Shane 'Shane Krzyzewski.'"

Jamal Boykin also lacked for Coach K's support. After leaving for Cal, he seemed to take a veiled shot at his former skipper.

"It's great to be a California Bear under Coach Braun, a coach who I believe in and I feel believes in me," Boykin said. "I look forward to continuing to build a great team with the players and coaches at Cal."

When Taylor King, who averaged a dismal 5.9 points and 2.0 rebounds in 2007–2008, left for greener pastures, Coach K—not surprisingly—supported the decision . . . though K couldn't resist twisting the knife one more time, telling *USA Today* that King "has the ability to be a good player." Not that he *had* been a good player, but that one day he *might* become one. King later complained of feeling "so burnt out" on college basketball.

Every school is going to have a player now and then that just doesn't fit in or has a higher sense of self than he should. But the trend in Durham is startling and no one asks why.

Whatever the reason, something is rotten in K-Ville.

Verdict: Guilty. When you can field three full teams from guys who've flown the coop, you've got a problem.

CHARGE #25

GIMME A P! GIMME AN L! GIMME AN A! GIMME AN I! GIMME AN N!

Look, occasionally we have to broach some unsavory topics around here. There's no way around it. We are soldiers of truth, and that's just the way we have to roll. It may sting for a moment, but hours, days, months from now, when you're laying in your bed, staring up at the ceiling, and pondering life's big questions, like what caused those rivulets in Shane Battier's head (lava?), you will thank us for our forthrightness.

So let's go ahead and rip off this Band-Aid.

Duke's cheerleaders are kind of butt.

Is that petty? Yes. Is it cheap? You know it. Is it sexist? Probably. But it doesn't make it any less true. And what's more, it's actually relevant, and as we've said, what we're trying to do here is figure out the reasons—*all* the reasons—why people may hate Duke. If the school consistently stocked the stands and sidelines with hotties, we guarantee you people would probably like Duke a lot more.

Ever seen a pretty woman get a speeding ticket? Of course not. Does anyone really hate Angelina Jolie, even though she's a man-stealing vampire, who makes out with her brother, and used to wear a vial of blood around her neck? They do not.

So, sorry to add to the already-rampant lookism in our society, but the Blue Devils cheerleaders are on the wrong side of hot. You know it, we know it, and former UNC coach Matt Doherty knows it.

During a 2001 Duke–UNC game, Doherty attempted to break the tension in a huddle by cracking to his team, "Oh, by the way, Duke still has the ugliest cheerleaders in the ACC."

It was an easy joke. Much like a rookie at an amateur comedy night might fall back on a quip about airline food or the way white people dance. And maybe it worked: UNC did win the game in the end.

Doherty went there, however, because the physical appearance of Duke's cheerleaders has been a running joke in Haterville for years. Just take a look for yourself during the next Cameron game. What do your eyes tell you? We will admit, though, that getting an accurate reading on something like hotness is difficult. This is not science. We know of no doctoral candidates studying the topic. We did, however, Google lots and lots of pictures of college cheerleaders (yes, we are total creeps who probably now have a file in the national sex-offender database), and there definitely appear to be much hotter cheerleaders at pretty much every other school in America.

But again, how do you keep stats on hotness?

You can't. What we can say is that there is certainly evidence out there that Duke isn't the first place anyone goes looking for the next supermodel. The 2009 *Playboy* edition of "Girls of the ACC" featured only one Duke girl. *The Chronicle* reported that just fifteen Duke coeds registered to attend the test-photo shoots compared to fifty to a hundred girls from other schools on average (according to a *Playboy* publicist). Even fewer reportedly showed up to have their photo taken. And the one girl who was selected to bare her Blue Devils was later seen in front of Perkins Library desperately asking passersby if they wanted a peek at her topless pics.

We are not making that up.

The Chronicle also tracked a former Duke girl who auditioned for the 2004 "Girls of the ACC" edition but—get this—her photos didn't make the cut. Her tots were turned away.

We can only find a total of four Duke cheerleaders who have ever been featured on SI.com's Cheerleader of the Week photo gallery. Oregon had that many just in the "Best of" Cheerleaders of the Week. Arizona State, UCLA, and Florida International (is that a University? We thought it was an airport.) had three in the "Best of," Minnesota had two, and TCU, UNC, Florida, Miami (OH), Georgia, USC, Texas, and Auburn had one each. Duke is nowhere to be found in the 2009 ranking of "Fifty Hottest Student Bodies" on the Web site popcrunch.com.

In March 2011, members of UNC's bench, collectively known as Blue Steel, caused controversy when they jokingly tweeted before a Duke–Carolina game in Chapel Hill, "How pumped are the Dook players to finally see some attractive people in the stands?"

"When Blue Steel comes out before the rest of the team to shoot around to get warmed up, a lot of times we'll spend that time scanning the court and stands for cheerleaders and good-looking girls. Just joking around with teammates," explains Blue Steel member Daniel Bolick. "And I remember specifically at Cameron, Blue Steel was talking together and mentioning how there were no attractive girls to be found. And we found one but she wasn't even a part of the Cameron Crazies, she was with the student news crew reporting on the game. It was a bunch of nerds in the Cameron Crazies. All the girls had their faces painted, but even the ones who didn't, we just couldn't really find any attractive girls who were in the stands."

The real question here is why? Is being around all that gawd-awful Gothic architecture slowly turning Dookies into gar-goyles? Do all of the hot girls from Jersey just move to the shore and star in reality shows instead of heading off to Duke?

Our conclusion is that it might just simply be a numbers game. Duke is the second smallest school in the ACC behind Wake Forest with only about six thousand undergraduate students. With the male/female split being about 50/50, that leaves only three thousand girls to choose from. Compare that to the thirty-two thousand undergrads at Florida State University and it's no wonder that FSU has a better chance of producing some-one like Jenn Sterger, a buxom booster who was known for at-tending Seminoles football games in tight clothing and a cowboy hat. A shot of her during a telecast caused ABC sportscaster Brent Musburger to exclaim on air, "I think fifteen hundred red-blooded American men just decided to go to FSU next se-mester." (And you thought *we* were creepy.) When Sterger later worked for the Jets, Brett Favre allegedly texted photos of his junk to her.

Can anyone at Duke say that? Then again, would they want to? Well played, Duke cheerleaders. Well played.

Verdict: Guilty, but with time off for good behavior and a promise to tame that unibrow.

EXHIBIT I

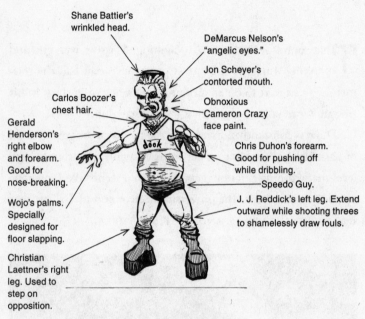

Shane Battier's wrinkled head.

DeMarcus Nelson's "angelic eyes."

Jon Scheyer's contorted mouth.

Carlos Boozer's chest hair.

Obnoxious Cameron Crazy face paint.

Gerald Henderson's right elbow and forearm. Good for nose-breaking.

Chris Duhon's forearm. Good for pushing off while dribbling.

Speedo Guy.

Wojo's palms. Specially designed for floor slapping.

J. J. Reddick's left leg. Extend outward while shooting threes to shamelessly draw fouls.

Christian Laettner's right leg. Used to step on opposition.

It's alive! And it just drew a suspect charge. Combine all the worst attributes of Duke players over the years, and you certainly have one helluva monster.
(Illustration by Joel Tesch)

CHARGE #26

GAAAAAAAAAAAAAK.

That sound you're hearing is choking. Massive, wet, guttural choking. Imagine the fattest guy you've ever had the misfortune to sit next to on an airplane with a hot wing stuck in his throat. We're talking about that level of gagging.

Duke is constantly portrayed in the media as the golden child of basketball, the team that performs at such a consistently high level that winning a national championship seems like a foregone conclusion each year. The university store once sold T-shirts that read DUKE BLUE DEVILS. AND THE FINAL THREE.

Cameron Crazies stain their facepaint with tears after a 2007 loss. *(Courtesy of Brian Allen)*

Shh, dry those tears. Your daddy is rich. *(Courtesey of Brian Allen)*

"I want Duke basketball to be good on a continuing basis," Krzyzewski says in his official bio. "All along it has been my goal to give Duke a program that will last, one that will be nationally ranked and worthy of postseason play every year."

The image of Duke's superiority has been so thoroughly drummed into our heads, that it's easy to take it for granted. Duke = winning. Always.

Until you stop and look at the actual numbers.

Let's examine Duke's recent performance in the NCAA tournament, because that's when the battle-hardened team and its revered leader should be showing its moxie. How many times would you guess they've made it to the Final Four from 2002 to 2011, just based on what your gut and Dick Vitale tell you? Three times? Four? Ten?

Try twice.

And those trips are far-and-away the anomalies. More often than not, Duke has flamed out spectacularly. We dare you to find a team that has more consistently underachieved during the past decade of postseason play.

"Duke's Underwhelming N.C.A.A. Run Continues" blared a 2009 *New York Times* headline after the Blue Devils were humiliated by the lower-seeded Villanova Wildcats.

In fact, it was the sixth year in a row that Duke had been upset by a lower-seeded opponent and the fifth consecutive year in which the Blue Devils failed to advance past the Sweet Sixteen.

What's worse was how many times Duke choked when they were a number one or number two seed. From 2002 to 2011, the team has lost four times in the Sweet Sixteen, despite entering as a top seed. That's like 1980s' Whitney Houston—pre-crack Whitney Houston—trying out for *American Idol* and not getting the golden ticket to Hollywood. Four times over.

As number two seeds, they bowed out early twice: in the Sweet Sixteen and in a 2008 second-round game to West Virginia.

And let's not even get into that 2007 first-round knockout by VCU—a school so overmatched on paper, it wouldn't even rate being called a David.

Not that any of these teams lacked talent. In 2006, for example, when the Blue Devils fizzled against LSU in the Sweet Sixteen, Coach K had on his roster the national and conference player of the year in J. J. Redick, the national and conference defensive player of the year in Shelden Williams, one of the most highly touted freshman and McDonald's All-American player of the year in Josh McRoberts, the Gatorade National High School Player of the Year in Greg Paulus, as well as former McDonald's

All-Americans Sean Dockery, DeMarcus Nelson, Lee Melchionni, and Eric Boateng. Failing to capitalize on that talent almost rises to the level of mismanagement. Sounds like Coach K is in line to run a bank next.

Winning a national championship even once in a decade is impressive, and Duke should be given its due. But let's not all pretend that Coach K and the Blue Devils have been fixtures in the Final Four and that the team has always lived up to its seeding or potential.

They haven't. Not even close. And there will always be a VCU, LSU, or Arizona to come along and slap us all back to reality.

Verdict: Anyone know the Heimlich?

EXHIBIT J

TOP 11 MOST HATED DUKE PLAYERS (BECAUSE A LIST OF 10 WAS JUST NOT ENOUGH)

J. J. REDICK

J. J. Redick—hated even in his hometown.
(Courtesy of Keith Allison)

2002–2006

Why he's awful: His own mother once dubbed him "the most hated college basketball player in the country." He was the picture of arrogance. He talked trash. He bobbed his head or threw up the lame shocker hand signal after nearly every made basket. He once slapped Chris Paul. Dude was a straight-up, pretty-boy punk. He's admitted that certain Carolina players, including Brendan Haywood, still won't talk to him in the NBA.

Current whereabouts: The shooting guard plays for Orlando, where he averaged 10.1 points for the 2010–2011 season. The supposed sharpshooter ranked fifty-ninth in the league in three-point percentage and thirty-eighth in free-throw percentage.

Fun fact: On a 2006 trip to Virginia Tech, Redick—who grew up nearby—was greeted with boos and a homemade sign reading, CAVE SPRINGS HATES J.J., referencing his high school.

MATT CHRISTENSEN
1996, 2000-2002

Why he's awful: The rage-filled meathead had a neck as thick as a telephone pole, and like so many Duke players, his contributions were inversely proportional to his celebratory antics. He averaged 1.5 points per game his senior year and 30 excited chest bumps. Students called the 265-pounder "the monster," and a vague unease often settled on the opposing fanbase when he entered a game, sure that someone was about to get headbutted.

Current whereabouts: Is now the CEO of Boston investment firm Rose Park Advisors, whose company Facebook page had exactly one "like" (when we last checked).

Fun fact: In a 2002 tournament loss to Indiana, Christensen had to be restrained from nearly punching the referee. He was reprimanded by the NCAA and had to write a letter of apology.

And what did Coach K do with Matt at the end of the year basketball banquet? Why, he gave him the Coach's Award, of course, which the *Duke Basketball Report* says goes to the "player exemplifying the commitment and values of Duke basketball." Okay, so the commitment and values of Duke Basketball mean almost punching a game official. Got it.

GREG PAULUS
2005–2009

Why he's awful: *Sports Illustrated* wrote in 2009 that "it's hard to remember a Blue Devil point guard as outmatched physically on the floor as Greg Paulus." His defense was suspect. He flopped even more than the average Dookie. He turned the rock over at an alarming rate. Even Blue Devils fans will admit they never loved him more than when he was benched his senior year in favor of Nolan Smith. Just another overhyped Blue Devil whose shortcomings were glossed over by endless sportscasters calling him "gritty." Kill us now.

Current whereabouts: When it became clear he had no future prospects in basketball, Paulus transferred to Syracuse to play football for one season. (He was often booed by Orange fans.) He tried out for the Saints in 2010 but was not offered a contract. He served one season as an assistant hoops coach at Navy before being let go. He was hired as a video coordinator at Ohio State in May 2011.

Fun fact: Even while on the sidelines at Navy, Paulus still got heckled. As an assistant coach! "They can say whatever they want to me," Paulus told *The Washington Post*. "I'm so accustomed to playing ACC road games and our nonconference schedule. It's really not a bother to me at all."

Danny Ferry
1985-1989

Why he's awful: He's like the missing link, in that all Duke hatred may stem from him. He was the original whiny, rich white boy. He got way too excited about each bucket. He may have scored 58 against Miami in 1988, the single-game record, but he completely flopped in the pros. A 1998 column in the *Akron Beacon Journal* noted, "His career always will be a disappointment, to both himself and the Cavs," then proceeded to run down the list of illustrious players Ferry had lost his job to: Mike Sanders, Tim Kempton, Winston Bennett, Henry James, and Cedric Henderson. Perhaps saddest of all, the six-foot-ten forward didn't dunk in at least the final six years of his career, according to league stats.

Current whereabouts: He became the VP of basketball operations for the San Antonio Spurs in 2010 after resigning as Cleveland's GM following the LeBron James debacle.

Fun fact: Him getting dunked on hard by NBA greats has inspired a miniseries on YouTube.

Christian Laettner
1988-1992

Why he's awful: He was an arrogant, insufferable douche in college, who often berated his teammates mercilessly on the court. Coach K once conceded that Chrissy was "first, second, and third" on the all-time most hated Dookies list. Things didn't improve much when Laettner was drafted by the Timberwolves. As the *St. Paul Pioneer Press* pointed out, Laettner was the most consistent player on the club: "He was hated by his teammates, assistant coaches, head coaches, medical staff, management personnel, ushers, janitors, popcorn vendors, and visiting clergy." He was suspended multiple times for bad behavior, before finally being shown the door after publicly criticizing his teammates. "Loser, loser, loser, loser . . ." he said, pointing to others' lockers. Of then-rookie Kevin Garnett, he said, "We've got some big britches on this team. We've got a lot of people who know everything." Whatever happened to that loser Garnett anyway?

Current whereabouts: He runs real estate company BD Ventures with former Duke teammate Brian Davis. The duo faced at least five lawsuits for failing to repay loans from friends and associates, including NFL linebacker Shawne Merriman. As of April 2011, the former Dookie was going begging for a job as an assistant coach.

Fun fact: Laettner finished his senior year one credit shy of graduating, and Coach K threatened to remove his retired jersey and the 1992 national championship banner from the rafters of Cameron if he didn't earn a degree over the summer.

CHRIS COLLINS
1993-1996

Why he's awful: He was the prototypical Duke punk-ass who perfectly filled the team's rich, white-boy quota with the departure of Hurley and Laettner. He was short with mediocre skills, and like a middle-aged dude who buys a convertible, Collins found a way to compensate. He overly celebrated and demonstrated enough faux-grit to endear himself to K forever. As an assistant coach, he nearly came to blows with then-UNC head coach Matt Doherty in 2003. (He would have gotten his ass kicked. Just saying.)

Current whereabouts: Sitting on the Duke bench as an assistant, saying "yes" to everything Coach K says.

Fun fact: He actually worked as an assistant in the WNBA before coaching at Duke.

Jay Williams
1999-2002

Why he's awful: Became K's golden child and the designated "dude that runs around eight screens per possession and jacks up as many threes as possible" guy. Picked second in the draft and promptly ruined his career and life. In 2003, he was riding a motorcycle through Chicago—helmetless, without a license, and in violation of his Chicago Bulls contract—when he crashed, severely injuring his leg.

Current whereabouts: Now working as a motivational speaker (seriously?), with an exaggerated bio that reads, "Mr. Williams parlayed a prolific basketball career at Duke University and the NBA into a successful career off the court." Prolific? He played one season for Chicago. Can also be found providing soul-deadening commentary on ESPN.

Fun fact: He has attempted multiple professional comebacks, most recently getting cut by the D-League Austin Toros after just three games in December 2006.

Bobby Hurley
1990–1993

Why he's awful: We'll concede that Bobby had mad skills. You don't set the career NCAA mark for assists without being above average. But for a guy whom David Teel of the *Daily Press* described as "previously an overwrought brat," he was known as an arrogant crier and complainer during his days at Duke. He even blatantly called out the officials following a loss to Iowa in January 1993, saying, "You wonder if the officials had a date after the game and didn't want to blow the whistles." (Imagine that: a Dookie complaining about not getting calls. Wow.)

Current whereabouts: Working as an assistant coach for his little brother Dan at Wagner College and doing commercials for Dove Men Care.

Fun fact: Just like his former teammate, Christian Laettner, Bobby has had some trouble with finances. In 2009, he was sued by PNC Bank in Lexington, Kentucky, for defaulting on a one-million-dollar loan.

Dahntay Jones
2001–2003

Why he's awful: Where do you even start with this Jersey native (surprise!) whose nicknames include "Dirtay" and "Tauntay"?

Like with the ethnic cleansing in Serbia or Snooki's novel, there are just too many awful incidents to choose from. "Dirtay" broke Wake Forest's Justin Gray's jaw while setting a screen. He cut Raymond Felton's chin with a wild elbow. He did showy push-ups for the TV camera after dunking on Virginia's Nick Vander Laan. After a jam near the end of the game, he taunted Larry Shyatt and the rest of the Clemson bench, which nearly caused a brawl.

Current whereabouts: Collecting flagrant and technical fouls galore for the NBA's Indiana Pacers.

Fun fact: Jones tried to transfer to UNC before heading to Duke, but Carolina had no scholarships available.

GERALD HENDERSON
2006-2009

Why he's awful: He broke Tyler Hansbrough's nose with his elbow. Coach K later protested that Gerald was the real victim of that play because he is such a "good kid." Was best friends with Wayne Ellington in high school yet still went to Duke.

Current whereabouts: Contributing mightily to the Charlotte Bobcats' eighty-six losses over his first two seasons in the NBA.

Fun fact: Both he and his father go by the name "Gerald," but that is not part of their given names of Jerome McKinley Henderson (Sr. and Jr.). What the hell is that all about?

AUSTIN RIVERS
2011-PRESENT

Why he's awful: Rivers, the son of Boston Celtics coach Doc Rivers, only arrived in Durham in fall 2011, but already this dude is on the fast train to becoming one of the all-time hated Duke players. In an extremely short-sighted comment in 2010, he said that UNC versus Duke is not that much of a rivalry because UNC needed to win more. I guess he overlooked the sweep from the previous season or the fact that Tyler Hansbrough won so frequently at Cameron from 2005 to 2009 (four straight) that it should be renamed Hansbrough Indoor Stadium. Oh, and Rivers also *gave himself* a nickname: Sub Zero. Terrible. Just terrible.

Current whereabouts: Probably driving one of the seniors on the team around, as Coach K demands.

Fun fact: Verbally committed to the University of Florida before changing his mind.

CHARGE #∞

The most difficult part about writing this book was finishing it, because as we all know, Duke suckitude never ends. The Blue Devils, Coach K, or one of those idiotic Crazies has probably done something terrible between the time you bought this book and when you got it home. To that end, please use this page to make any additions to this book you see fit.

Thanks,
—The Management

AFTERWORD

So here we are. We've finally come to the end of our sometimes ugly, sometimes exhilarating, occasionally upsetting journey. We have strapped on our miner's hats and explored every dark crevice of Duke basketball. And what have we learned?

That's the big question, after all. It's the question that everyone who has encountered this phenomenon of Duke hatred—from coaches to players to journalists to that chick the team's Casey Sanders was accused of assaulting—has endlessly wondered. How did this happen? Why is one team in America detested above all others, seemingly irrespective of a fan's conference affiliation, geographic location, gender, race, or age?

We've run down dozens of individual reasons why people don't like Duke, and for certain fans, maybe one of those reasons is enough. But culturally, something bigger must be going on. Duke hatred on this scale can't possibly stem from a single stray elbow, a blown call by an official, or an F-bomb by Coach K, no matter how terrible those things are taken alone.

No, this phenomenon has to be about something more than that. There must be something about Duke that really pushes our subconscious buttons, that disturbs us on a much deeper level. Something that is more important and less superficial than a single, fleeting basketball game. The pain of a loss is gone in a matter of hours, maybe days, but the grudge even casual basketball fans seem to have against Duke can last a lifetime.

So what is it that many of the gripes against Duke have in common?

If you ask us, it all boils down to one single thing: unfairness.

The Duke basketball team offends one of the most sacred of American beliefs. It offends our sense of justice.

This country was supposedly built on the principles of a square deal and equality for all. If you work hard, so the belief goes, you will be rewarded. Duke takes that sacred principle and drops a steaming pile on it.

The Blue Devils are doing nothing short of sullying the American dream.

Think about the reason you hate Duke most. Reduced to its simplest level, it probably comes down to a feeling that they're getting away with something, that they're being treated differently than other teams, and that is what is so galling.

Plenty of programs have had potential NCAA violations, for example. That's not the part that irks us. The part that irks us—and we're betting you—is Duke rarely gets held accountable for violations by the league or gets called on them by the media.

Plenty of programs are run by world-class assholes. That doesn't necessarily anger us. What angers us is that Coach K is never treated as anything less than an infallible saint by the university and the media. Remember that magazine cover talking about how Coach K was "what's right with sports"?

We don't like that Duke gets calls. But what we like even less is the hypocrisy of Coach K whining that Dean Smith was getting preferential treatment.

Other players may flop. But Duke players seem to get away with it more often, especially at critical moments in a game.

Duke basketball fans are obnoxious and not particularly loyal, especially when it comes to other sport programs on campus. But what really pisses people off about them is that they continue to coast on their perpetual reputation (enabled by the media) as the best fans in the game, despite reams of evidence to the contrary.

And on and on and on.

Duke is basically the JP Morgan-Chase-Bank of America-Barclays of the college-sporting world. It has virtually unlimited power, money, and influence, which it uses to recruit top players, earn calls, steamroll opponents, and tightly control its image in the media. Then it sits back and summons mock outrage at the suggestion that the playing field could possibly be tilted in its favor.

The little guy doesn't have a prayer, and that's what makes this so un-American. We believe and demand fairness in this country. We don't dislike rich people, for example. We dislike rich people who trash the economy, trample on everyone else, then retire to their yacht in the Caribbean while the authorities do nothing. We don't hate paying taxes in principle; we hate paying taxes because we have the suspicion that the system—with its endless write-offs and loopholes—is rigged in favor of those wealthier and more powerful than the rest of us.

That same type of populist rage that was turned on, say, Goldman Sachs, is what has been directed at Duke all these years. We don't hate them because they win, despite what the team will try to tell you. We don't hate them because their student body is wealthier, more entitled, and more insufferable than most. (Although that doesn't help.) We hate them because they're like the fat cats who get special treatment.

The motto of the state of North Carolina is *"Esse quam videri."* It's a Latin phrase than basically means, "To be, rather than to seem to be." It's about image versus reality, and the gap between the idealized version of Duke that is presented to us and the actual reality is so wide, you could drive Chris Duhon's sweet Altima through it.

It's time to recognize this gap. It's time for everyone to acknowledge reality, and that means fans, the media, and Duke University itself. The only way to repair the program's image and stop building legions of new haters every season is through honesty, self-awareness, and transparency on everyone's part.

That and to stop recruiting those worthless Plumlees. Jesus, those guys totally suck.

ABOUT THE AUTHORS

Reed Tucker and Andy Bagwell produce the popular weekly podcast Tar Heel Bred, Tar Heel Dead (thbthd.com), a thorough, occasionally humorous analysis of UNC hoops. Tucker is a staff writer at the *New York Post* and lives in Brooklyn. Bagwell is a former member of Selected Hilarity, one of the top college comedy acts in the nation, and lives in North Carolina.